JOURNEYS

Road Map to Success

Write-In Reader
Grade 6

Printed in the U.S.A.

ISBN: 978-0-547-25425-8

123456789- 0877- 17 16 15 14 13 12 11 10 09

HOUGHTON MIFFLIN HARCOURT
School Publishers

Contents

✓ TARGET VOCABULARY

disclose
muted
pressuring
revisions
wry

A Poetry Contest

1 My school was having a poetry contest. The best poem in each class would be published in our school newspaper. Students weren't required to submit a poem, but my friend Emil was **pressuring** me to write one. He knew that I loved poetry.

Tell about a time when someone was <u>pressuring</u> you to do better work in school or in sports.

_____

_____

_____

2 One rule was that the author of each poem must not **disclose** his or her identity until after the voting. Everyone in the class would get a vote. Our principal wanted to make sure that students voted on the poems without being influenced by who wrote them.

Write a synonym of <u>disclose</u>.

_____

3 I wrote about a rainstorm that had flooded our basement and ruined some family photographs. Parts of the poem were funny. My parents told me that I had a **wry** sense of humor to be able to joke about something so serious.

Describe another situation where you could make a <u>wry</u> joke.

_____

_____

_____

4 I worked hard on my poem and made several **revisions**. I changed some of the rhymes and punctuation until my poem sounded just right.

What kinds of <u>revisions</u> might you make to an essay about your favorite author?

_____

_____

_____

5 Before I handed in the poem, I read it to myself. I **muted** my voice so that no one else could hear. I was happy with my poem, regardless of whether or not it would be published in the school paper!

Tell about a time when you <u>muted</u> your voice. Why did you speak quietly?

_____

_____

_____

My Poems

Song for the Whales

by Mia Lewis

Every year, the whales stopped in our cove during their six-thousand-mile trip south from the Bering Sea. They always seemed to be traveling slowly, as if they had all the time in the world. They swam right into the cove next to our town and stayed there for days. You could see them splashing their tails and looking at everyone on the beach.

People came from far away to see those huge and amazing creatures. Binoculars in hand, spectators stood on the sand and gazed out at the whales. The whales seemed to like the attention. They would dive and spout water almost as if they were performing for us. I couldn't imagine feeling so comfortable with all those people watching me. Just the idea of performing made me freeze up like a block of ice.

Stop Think Write

UNDERSTANDING CHARACTERS

What do the whales seem to be able to do that the narrator cannot?

_____

_____

_____

I loved spending time at the cove, but I usually went when no one else was around. You see, the beach was a great spot to write my songs. I sat on the rocks with my notebook and wrote down tunes and lyrics. I don't think I could have written a word if I thought someone might be looking over my shoulder. However, sitting by myself next to the sea, I sometimes wrote for hours. No one was **pressuring** me to work faster. I could make as many **revisions** as I wanted before a song was finished.

After I wrote the songs, I tried singing them. I felt too shy to sing in front of people, but the whales were a great audience! They swam and jumped in the cove while I sang. They seemed to like my songs, and I knew they would never **disclose** my secret. I hadn't told my family or friends about my songs. I wasn't ready to share my music yet. I wasn't sure I'd ever be ready.

Stop | Think | Write

VOCABULARY

Describe a time when someone wanted you to <u>disclose</u> information.

_____

_____

_____

5

While I was walking along the rocks one day, I spotted an odd shape in the water next to the beach. It was a whale! I saw right away that the whale was in trouble. It wasn't diving or splashing or blowing water. In fact, the whale wasn't moving at all, and much of it was out of the water. I realized that it must have swum too close to the shore and gotten stuck. A whale out of water was a bad thing, because whales need to stay wet. I knew I wasn't big enough to push the whale out to deeper water. Still, I had to do something, so I turned and ran back down the beach for help.

I spotted my sister Rosa coming toward me. "Rosa!" I yelled frantically. "Quick, go home and get help—a whale is stuck on the beach!"

Rosa hesitated for a second, then turned and ran toward home. I stayed with the whale to keep watch.

Stop Think Write

CONCLUSIONS AND GENERALIZATIONS

How does the narrator know that the whale is in trouble?

_____

_____

_____

A few minutes later, my mom and dad came rushing toward me, with Rosa close on their heels. I showed them where the whale was, and we all walked toward it. Even though it was stuck, I could tell the whale was alive. It seemed to be watching us, and the air hole on top of its head moved as it breathed. Being so close to such a huge and powerful creature was scary, but also exciting. I hoped we could help it.

"We need to get this whale back in the sea!" Dad said. "Tomás, you and Rosa keep the whale wet while we run and get help."

Rosa and I waded into the water next to the whale and began to splash it.

"Oh, I wish the tide would hurry up and come in!" Rosa said.

I felt impatient, too, but I knew that the tide hurried for no one. "It won't be high tide for several hours," I told her. "We'll just have to wait."

Stop · Think · Write

UNDERSTANDING CHARACTERS

What do Tomás's and Rosa's actions tell you about them?

_____

_____

_____

The whale's look tormented me. Even though Rosa and I were keeping it wet, the whale was trembling with fear. I didn't see what else we could do to help it. Then I looked out at the other whales in the cove. They made me think of my songs and how much the whales seemed to like them. An idea took shape in my head.

"I'll sing to it!" I said to Rosa.

"You sing?" Rosa asked, shooting a puzzled glance at me.

At first I **muted** my voice and sang so quietly that I was making hardly any sound at all.

"Sing louder, Tomás. I think the whale is relaxing!" Rosa said.

So I sang louder. The whale *did* seem more relaxed. It wasn't trembling as much anymore, and a subtle twitch of its tail fin let me know that it was still alive. Rosa and I kept splashing the whale with water as I sang my songs.

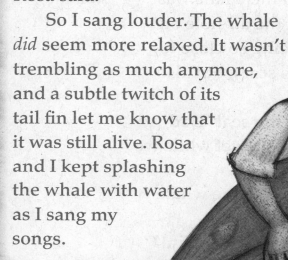

Stop	**Think**	**Write**

VOCABULARY

Why might Tomás have <u>muted</u> his voice to sing to the whale?

_____

_____

_____

A while later, we heard voices coming down the beach. My parents were back, and they were bringing help—lots of it, from what I could tell! It seemed as if the entire town had come to help save the whale.

I continued singing while everyone helped keep the whale wet. Whenever the whale started to shiver, I made my song softer to calm it down. I didn't think about the other people, or even look at them. I just thought about keeping the whale calm and alive until we could help it get to deeper water.

You know what? The more I sang, the calmer the whale seemed. The other whales in the cove seemed to be listening, too. They swam and splashed as they always did when I sang. I thought they might be watching and waiting for their friend to rejoin them.

Stop Think Write

UNDERSTANDING CHARACTERS

Why doesn't Tomás think about or look at the other people?

_____

_____

_____

At last the tide reached its highest point. The water lifted our whale from the sand, and it struggled out into the cove. I breathed a sigh of relief to see it swim off, safe and free.

As it joined the other whales, we all began to clap. It took me a moment to realize that the people around me didn't stop clapping when I did. With shock, I realized that they were now clapping for me!

"How on earth did you make up those amazing songs?" asked my mom.

When I described how I spent my time alone on the beach, my family was astonished.

"Keep writing your songs, Tomás," said my dad with pride. "Don't sing them just to save the whales," he added with a wry smile. "We'd like to hear them, too!"

I had thought it would be embarrassing to share my songs, but it made me feel good. In fact, it made me feel great!

"Okay," I agreed. "You've got a deal."

Stop | **Think** | **Write**

UNDERSTANDING CHARACTERS

Does Tomás's family like his songs? How can you tell?

_____

_____

_____

Look Back and Respond

1 How does Tomás feel about sharing his songs at the beginning of the story?

Hint

For clues, look on pages 4 and 5.

_____

_____

_____

2 How does Tomás change at the end of the story?

Hint

For clues, look at pages 4, 5, 9, and 10.

_____

_____

_____

3 Why does Tomás change his mind about singing his songs in front of other people?

Hint

For clues, see page 10.

_____

_____

_____

4 Why is Tomás shocked to realize that people are clapping for him?

Hint

For clues, see pages 5 and 10.

_____

_____

_____

11

✓ TARGET VOCABULARY

culprit
deprived
grimly
miraculous
pursuit

Turning Life Into Art

Some people write stories about their lives. Other people make movies or take photographs that document important personal events. People make sculptures and paintings about their experiences, too. Their lives become part of their

1 _____ of interesting and beautiful art.

Even difficult situations can give you material for something creative. Let's say that your favorite pen disappears. You think someone might have taken it, and you search for the

2 _____. You may think **3** _____ of classmates who sit near your desk. It could turn out that you simply misplaced the pen, or that someone took it accidentally. Even so, you could write an intriguing mystery based on the experience, or make a painting about it.

People should not be

4 _____ of the opportunity to express themselves creatively. When you make a film or a series of photographs about something personal, the results can be amazing, or even

5 _____!

The Great Basketball Movie

by Richard Stull

"What are we going to do, Eddie?" asked Kenny.

Kenny and I were standing in the Middletown gym, watching our teammates practice basketball. Well, they were trying to practice. None of us really knew how to play basketball. In fact, none of us even liked basketball. However, for two days we had practiced, **grimly** determined to convince ourselves that we could play. How crazy could you get?

The madness started last week. That's when Middletown's inter-club games had been announced. The games were a school tradition that took place every year. Each after-school club was assigned to play some sort of sports game against another club. Usually, the game was no big deal. None of the clubs cared who won. We showed up for the game, had a little fun, and went home.

Stop | Think | Write

VOCABULARY

What task do you have to do that you perform <u>grimly</u>? Explain.

_____

_____

_____

14

Filmmaker's Club
to play...
Fantasy Sports Club
Tickets

Advance: $5.00

At the door: $6.00

This year, though, things were different. The chosen sport was basketball. Our club, the Filmmakers Club, was picked to play the Fantasy Sports Club. That's where the trouble began. We cared mostly about movies. We didn't think much about basketball. The kids in the Fantasy Sports Club were different. Even though they didn't all play basketball, they took sports seriously… very seriously.

The kids in Fantasy Sports knew a lot more about basketball than we ever would. A few of them were excellent players, too. They really wanted to win the game. Furthermore, they expected us to show up and play hard. They made it clear that they would consider anything less than a hard-fought game a form of treachery. They had no intention of being **deprived** of a meaningful victory.

Stop Think Write

MAIN IDEAS AND DETAILS

Do you think the game between the two clubs will be a close game? Give two details that support your thinking.

_____

_____

_____

I sighed. Kenny and I jogged out onto the gym floor to join the practice. Here we were, the five of us: Kenny, Ana, Jamal, Mai, and me, Eddie. I tossed the ball to Kenny. "Why don't you practice dribbling," I said.

Kenny started bouncing the ball across the floor. Mai covered her face with her hands. "No, Kenny," she shouted. "You have to use one hand to dribble, not two."

We were hopeless. There was no denying it. Nothing short of a **miraculous** game would save us. I decided that we needed a creative game plan—fast. I searched for some inspiration. I began to imagine the game as a scene in a movie I was directing. I wondered how I would approach the scene.

Stop | Think | Write

Why do you think the author includes the scene of Kenny dribbling the basketball with two hands?

_____

_____

_____

Snap! In an instant I had an idea. We would turn our pathetic attempt to play a basketball game into a documentary film. I could see it in my mind. It would be the story of five ordinary kids sent cruelly to their doom on a basketball court. It would be a huge hit!

"Hey, everyone," I called out. "Come over for a huddle. I've got a great idea." My four teammates walked over. Mai pointed out that basketball players don't really huddle, but we did anyway.

"Okay," Kenny said. "What's your bright idea for making us a winning team?"

"Not a winning team," I said. "We're not even going to try to win. Instead, we're going to turn our loss into a documentary film about the losing team, us."

"A film about losers?" Jamal asked. "Hey, I kind of like the sound of that."

Stop | Think | Write

STORY STRUCTURE

What is Eddie's plan to help his team?

_____

_____

_____

17

"Won't the kids in Fantasy Sports get angry?" asked Mai. "If we don't even try, they're bound to blame us for robbing them of their moment of glory. I don't want them to see our team as the **culprit**."

"Maybe they won't be sore," I said. "After all, they'll be in the movie, too. At least this way, they'll get something exciting out of the game. Of course, I don't think we should tell them that we plan to lose."

"Yeah, let's not mention that point," Kenny agreed. "We'll just ask them if they want to be in the movie. They can accept or reject the idea."

Of course, the Fantasy members were delighted to be part of our movie. They imagined a thrilling saga of a hard-fought game between two evenly matched teams. In other words, they didn't know the truth.

| Stop | Think | Write |

CAUSE AND EFFECT

Why don't Eddie and his friends want to tell the members of Fantasy Sports that they plan to lose?

_____

_____

_____

I felt bad about what we were doing. I told myself that a little deception is often needed in **pursuit** of a good movie. Kenny loaded the camera, and we all got to work. We interviewed the kids in Fantasy Sports. They talked about how excited they were about the upcoming game. Then we interviewed each other. We talked about how important losing would be to each of us.

On the day of the game, Kenny's brother stood on the sidelines with the camera, filming the game. He got lots of great shots. He filmed Kenny putting up a one-handed shot into the wrong basket. He also shot Jamal grabbing the ball out of Ana's hands. I guess Jamal had forgotten that she was on our team.

Needless to say, the Fantasy Sports Club whipped us. The final score was 37–12. Afterward, I could tell that they were really angry. They felt we had embarrassed them by not taking the game seriously. It was hard to argue.

Stop | Think | Write

How do Eddie and his friends use deception in pursuit of a good movie?

_____

_____

_____

Later that week, we held a screening of our movie. Of course, we invited the kids in Fantasy.

Everyone sat silently while the film was screened. I must admit that I was impressed with our work. The movie was funny, with a lot of fake "serious" interviews with our teammates talking about how meaningful losing was to us. These were included with scenes from the game and scenes of the Fantasy Sports Club talking about winning.

With some great background music and funny titles, the film was a success. Even the members of Fantasy agreed. "I have to hand it to you," one of them said, "You may stink at basketball, but you sure make great movies."

The Fantasy Sports Club huddled together, and then yelled out a cheer. "Let's hear it for the losers!" they shouted. It was music to my ears.

Stop | Think | Write

AUTHOR'S PURPOSE

Why do you think the author ends the selection by having the Fantasy Sports Club cheer Eddie and his friends?

_____

_____

_____

Look Back and Respond

1 Why do you think the author wrote this story?

_____

_____

_____

Hint
What is the message of the story?

2 How would you describe Eddie?

_____

_____

_____

Hint
Clues appear on almost every page.

3 Why are the members of the Fantasy Sports Club team angry after the basketball game?

_____

_____

_____

Hint
For clues, see pages 15, 18, and 19.

4 Do you think the author of *The Great Basketball Movie* approves of Eddie's plan? Explain.

_____

_____

_____

Hint
For clues, see pages 17 through 20.

Lesson 3

✓ TARGET VOCABULARY

conclusion
emphatically
manipulated
precisely
resolve

Writing an Essay

The first step to writing a good essay is planning. You need more than just a vague idea of the topic. You must decide **precisely** what your essay will be about. What main idea do you want to get across? What specific information would you like to include?

Let's say you want to write about how you **manipulated** clay to make a sculpture. First, you must organize your ideas. Think about which details you want to include. Plan the order in which you will present the information. What **conclusion** will you make about the process of making a clay sculpture? Make an outline with notes about what you will write and how you will organize the information.

You will use the outline to write your essay. Then it's time to edit. Does your writing make sense? Is the information organized logically? Could you add or cut any details? If there are problems with grammar or spelling, now is the time to **resolve** them.

Take a final look at your essay. Can you say **emphatically** that the essay meets your goals? If so, then it is done.

1 Before writing an essay, you must decide _____ what the topic of the essay will be.

2 When you speak _____ about a topic, you give great force to your words.

3 The information in your essay may lead to a _____ that you make at the end of the essay.

4 When you edit your essay, you should try to _____ problems such as spelling and grammar mistakes.

5 Tell about a time when you <u>manipulated</u> something.

_____

_____

_____

6 Write a synonym for <u>precisely</u>.

_____

What's My Talent?

by Estelle Kleinman

Everyone in my class groaned as we packed up our backpacks for the long holiday weekend. Our English teacher had actually given us homework. We were supposed to write an essay about a talent we have that makes us happy.

"I **hate** this assignment!" I said emphatically to one of my classmates. I couldn't think of a single thing to write about.

On the way home from school, I thought about the essay. I knew that we would have to read our essays out loud. I thought, *What am I good enough at doing that I can write about, read aloud, and not make the whole class break out in hysterics?*

Maybe I could write about being a math whiz. I'm almost as good as my math teacher at figuring out difficult problems. I'm also an excellent speller. However, neither of those talents made me happy enough to write about it.

Stop | Think | Write

TEXT AND GRAPHIC FEATURES

Why does the writer put the word "hate" in bold (dark and heavy) type?

_____

_____

_____

On Sunday, I still didn't know what to write about. My family and I were on our way to a family reunion, and I had low expectations of having any fun. Most of the cousins my age weren't going, so I prepared myself to be bored all day.

Can things get any worse? I thought.

The reunion was at a big park. A small crowd had gathered under a pavilion. I cringed when someone decided that we should play games. When it comes to sports, I have two left feet. I stood along the fringes of the group. I tried to be invisible, but it didn't work. I had to play anyway.

I escaped as soon as possible and started to look for rocks for my rock collection. When I got tired of that, Uncle Charles and I played a game of chess. That kept me busy for a while.

Stop **Think** **Write**

MAIN IDEAS AND DETAILS

Why does the narrator try to hide when teams are being chosen?

_____

_____

_____

It was still early, so I began to look around for other kids to play with. I saw two kids with their parents. They looked to be about five and seven. In other words, they were too young for me to hang out with. Still, I walked over to them. The five-year-old clung to her mother.

"Hello," I said. "I'm David. What are your names?"

The children looked at me blankly. Then their mother said, with a thick accent, "This is Alexander, and this is Sonia."

Now I understood. These were my relatives who had recently moved from Russia. The children didn't speak English, and I certainly didn't speak Russian! I wasn't sure how to **resolve** this problem.

Then an idea came to me. The surface of a pond glimmered a few yards away, and I coaxed Alexander to follow me to the water's edge.

Stop | Think | Write

How do you think that David might <u>resolve</u> his problem?

_____

_____

_____

I picked up a stone, aimed it at an angle, and threw it across the water. I **manipulated** the stone in such a way that it skimmed the surface. It jumped three times, and then plopped into the water. Not bad!

Alexander squealed with pleasure. I picked up a rock and handed it to him. He threw it across the water just as I had done. The stone skipped once. He looked up and grinned. By this time, Sonia had joined us.

"I know. We'll play hide-and-seek," I told them. From my motions, they understood exactly what to do. I guessed that they knew how to play hide-and-seek. We laughed as we chased each other.

After lunch, I got some drawing paper from the car, along with colored pens. I called the kids over to a table, and they came eagerly. First, I drew a squiggly black line on the paper. Then I took a colored pen and completed the picture to make a smiley face, with the squiggly line becoming the smile.

Stop · Think · Write

TEXT AND GRAPHIC FEATURES

What is the purpose of the illustrations on this page?

_____

_____

_____

Now it was their turn. I took out two fresh pieces of paper and drew two jagged lines, one on each paper.

I gave the colored pens to Alexander and Sonia. Both of them were creative, and the squiggles soon became pictures!

Before I knew it, the reunion was over, and everyone was going home. Sonia and Alexander's parents came to fetch them, but they hid behind me, giggling.

Their mother said, "We were so worried that Sonia and Alexander would not have anyone to play with. Thank you for entertaining them. You have a great gift for taking care of children."

"It was no problem," I said. "They made the party fun for me, too." I meant it, too. I had really enjoyed myself.

Stop **Think** **Write**

INFER AND PREDICT

Why does the children's mother tell David that he has a gift for taking care of children?

_____

_____

_____

On the way home, I had a vague idea for my essay. I would write about the reunion. *Just how will I tell the story?* I wondered.

Should I tell about the soccer game? I didn't show much talent there. I fell twice and never scored a goal. I decided that the less said about that game the better.

I thought about describing how I looked for rocks for my collection. I imagined how I might present this to my classmates. I could practically hear my classmates snoring.

What else? Oh, yes, I could write about the chess game, but that might bring on snoring, too. I really didn't want to face the possibility of that kind of humiliation.

Then I thought about Alexander and Sonia. Playing with them had made me happy. Their mother said I had a great gift. I didn't know about that, but now I knew **precisely** what I'd write about—the time I spent with the children.

Stop Think Write

COMPARE AND CONTRAST

How does David's reason for not writing about soccer differ from his reason for not writing about chess?

_____

_____

_____

Journal Entry—May 26

Today at school, I stood up and read my essay to the class. I told about the day I spent at my family reunion and how I had thought that it would be dreadful. Instead, it turned out to be a great day, thanks to Alexander and Sonia.

When I got home, I read the essay to my parents. After I finished, my father smiled and said how proud of me he was. He said that being good with children was a much better gift than being the best soccer player on the field.

I don't know whether his **conclusion** is right, but I know that hearing it made me feel good. I also know that my essay was not a disaster. Who knows? Maybe I have other talents I don't even know about yet.

Stop   Think   Write

What <u>conclusion</u> does David's father reach?

_____

_____

_____

Look Back and Respond

1 In the story, some sentences are shown in italics (a special sloping typeface). Why are these sentences in italics?

_____

_____

_____

Hint

For clues, see pages 24, 25, and 29.

2 Why does David decide to write his essay about the time he spent with Sonia and Alexander?

_____

_____

_____

Hint

For a clue, see pages 24 and 29.

3 What lets you know that the last page of the story is different from the rest of the story? Why do you think the author chose to do this?

_____

_____

_____

Hint

Look at page 30. What does the heading tell you about the text that follows?

4 What do you think the author's most important points are?

_____

_____

_____

Hint

Look for clues on page 30.

accustomed
clustered
coaxed
urgent
void

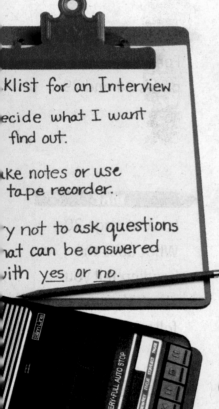

klist for an Interview

ecide what I want
find out.

ke notes or use
tape recorder.

y not to ask questions
at can be answered
ith yes or no.

Stories All Around

Check the answer.

1 Everyone has a story to tell, but we don't always take the time to listen. You might be _____ to saying hello to your neighbors, but have you taken the time to really get to know them?

☐ **clustered** ☐ **employed** ☐ **accustomed**

2 If you have a _____ in your day, you can fill the empty time by asking your neighbors about themselves.

☐ **void** ☐ **culprit** ☐ **coaxed**

3 People may be shy about sharing their stories at first. However, they may become more comfortable as you get to know them. Once people have been _____ into talking about themselves, they usually like it!

☐ **accustomed** ☐ **coaxed** ☐ **clustered**

4 Some people are bursting with stories that they just have to share! Someone might have an _____ need to talk about a particular experience or about a person who changed his or her life.

☐ **urgent** ☐ **revolting** ☐ **accustomed**

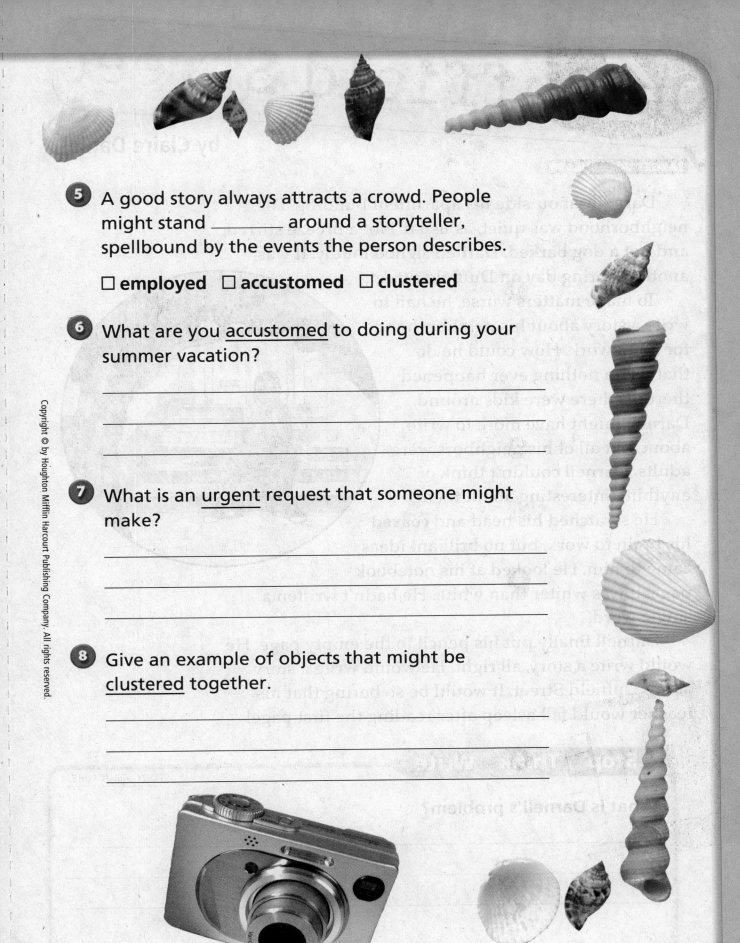

5 A good story always attracts a crowd. People might stand _____ around a storyteller, spellbound by the events the person describes.

☐ **employed**   ☐ **accustomed**   ☐ **clustered**

6 What are you <u>accustomed</u> to doing during your summer vacation?

_____

_____

_____

7 What is an <u>urgent</u> request that someone might make?

_____

_____

_____

8 Give an example of objects that might be <u>clustered</u> together.

_____

_____

_____

On Duffield Street

by Claire Daniel

Darnell sat outside his apartment building. The neighborhood was quiet, as usual. Not a breeze stirred, and not a dog barked. Darnell sighed loudly. It was another boring day on Duffield Street.

To make matters worse, he had to write a story about his neighborhood for homework. How could he do that when nothing ever happened there? If there were kids around, Darnell might have more to write about, but all of his neighbors were adults. Darnell couldn't think of anything interesting about them.

He scratched his head and **coaxed** his brain to work, but no brilliant ideas came to him. He looked at his notebook page. It was whiter than white. He hadn't written a single word.

Darnell finally put his pencil to the empty page. He would write a story, all right. He would write a story about Duffield Street. It would be so boring that his teacher would fall asleep after reading the first page!

Stop | Think | Write

STORY STRUCTURE

What is Darnell's problem?

_____

_____

_____

Darnell saw his neighbor, Mr. Angelo, walking toward him. Every day, Mr. Angelo stopped on his way to his favorite cafe and tried to chat with Darnell. The old man always went on and on. Darnell usually said he had something **urgent** to do, because he didn't want to listen.

"Hi, Darnell," Mr. Angelo said. "What are you writing?"

"A story about the neighborhood," Darnell said. He hoped Mr. Angelo would keep walking, but he stopped.

"I have a million stories about this block!" Mr. Angelo said. "My favorite one is about my mother and father after they got married."

Darnell thought, "Here he goes again," but he didn't say the words out loud.

"My parents were born in Italy, but they met here in America," Mr. Angelo went on. "Then World War II started up, and Dad joined the army. My mom was all alone. It was lucky for her that she met Pauline."

Stop   Think   Write

Why does Darnell usually say he has something <u>urgent</u> to do when Mr. Angelo tries to talk to him?

_____

_____

_____

"Pauline? The lady who used to run the café?" Darnell asked. Pauline's had been on the block for as long as he could remember. The gray-haired lady who ran the place had retired just the year before. Now her son ran Pauline's.

Mr. Angelo nodded and said, "Yes, except Pauline's wasn't here when Mama and Papa came to this block. When Papa left, Mama was miserable. She felt a **void** in her life. She was **accustomed** to her large Italian family, and now she was alone with a little toddler to care for."

"You?" Darnell asked.

"Yes. Pauline saw how sad my mother was," Mr. Angelo went on. "The two became best friends. Then Pauline came up with a plan that changed their lives."

Stop **Think** **Write**

STORY STRUCTURE

What is Mr. Angelo's mother's problem?

_____

_____

_____

"What was the plan?" Darnell asked. He leaned forward, listening closely. He could hardly believe it, but Angelo's story was actually interesting!

Mr. Angelo said, "Pauline came up with the idea of a restaurant. She was a very good cook, and so was my mother. They decided to start a business cooking large family meals for everyone in the neighborhood."

"Where was the restaurant?" Darnell asked.

"At first, they set up tables in Pauline's living room," said Mr. Angelo. "Then that got too crowded, so they decided to rent a space down at the end of the street. I think you know where that restaurant is!"

"The same place where Pauline's is now?" asked Darnell. "That's where you eat lunch every day, isn't it?"

"Right you are!" Mr. Angelo said, nodding. "On the very first day they opened, many people came to eat. The dining room was filled with diners! In short, Pauline's plan was a great success."

Stop Think Write

STORY STRUCTURE

How might Pauline's plan solve the problem that Mr. Angelo's mother has?

_____

_____

_____

"Then what happened?" Darnell asked.

"Well," said Mr. Angelo, "Mama always sang to herself while she worked. She had a lovely voice, and one day, Pauline asked her to sing for the customers. Mama picked out a few songs, and they hired a piano player. My mother became quite a hit. People started coming to the restaurant both to eat the good food and to hear my mother sing. Sometimes it was so crowded that people **clustered** in the doorway to hear Mama."

"Your mother must have been a very good singer," Darnell said.

"Oh, yes," Mr. Angelo said proudly.

"Your mother wasn't sad anymore about your dad being gone?" Darnell asked.

"She was a little sad," said Mr. Angelo. "I was very little, but I remember that she was busy all the time. She probably didn't have time to feel too alone."

Stop | Think | Write

Why were people clustered in the doorway of the restaurant?

_____

_____

_____

Mr. Angelo continued, "Mama loved singing, and she liked cooking the dinners because it was like cooking for her big family in Italy. The people in this neighborhood were like a new family to her. Then, when my father came home, my mother had a huge surprise. She had made a lot of money from the restaurant. She and Papa had enough to buy an apartment right on this block."

"The same one where you live now?" Darnell asked.

"Yes, indeed!" Mr. Angelo said. "My mother worked at Pauline's for many years. I like going there to eat because it's like eating Mama's home cooking."

"Mr. Angelo, that is a great story," Darnell said. "Why haven't you told it to me before?"

Darnell felt his face get hot. He knew the answer to his question. He had heard Mr. Angelo talk before, but he had never really listened to what he had to say.

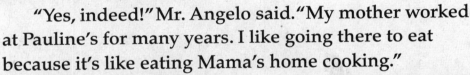

Stop | Think | Write

INFER AND PREDICT

Why does Darnell's face feel hot?

_____

_____

_____

Mr. Angelo smiled at Darnell. "Any time you want a story," he said, "you know where to find one. I'll be glad to tell you anything you want to know."

Mr. Angelo continued walking toward Pauline's. After he left, Darnell sat down and began to write. His pencil moved quickly on the paper. When he was done, an idea came to him. Maybe he could talk to Pauline! She might have more to add to the story.

Darnell looked at his street with new eyes. Suddenly, Duffield Street seemed much more interesting. So did Mr. Angelo. For all Darnell knew, his other neighbors knew more stories like the one Mr. Angelo had told him. All Darnell had to do was ask—and then listen to what people told him.

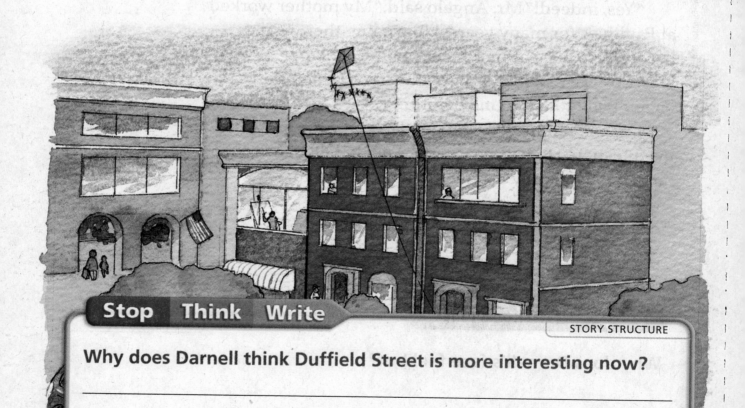

Stop **Think** **Write**

Why does Darnell think Duffield Street is more interesting now?

_____

_____

_____

Look Back and Respond

1 *On Duffield Street* has a story within a story. What are the two stories?

_____

_____

_____

Hint

Think about Darnell's situation. Think about what Mr. Angelo tells Darnell.

2 Who are the main characters in the story that Mr. Angelo tells Darnell?

_____

_____

_____

Hint

For clues, look on pages 36 and 37.

3 Why doesn't Darnell want to listen to Mr. Angelo in the beginning of the story?

_____

_____

_____

Hint

For clues, look on page 35.

4 How does Darnell change from the beginning of the story to the end?

_____

_____

_____

Hint

For clues, see pages 34 and 40.

aspect
credit
genuinely
tendency
tension

Becoming a Comedian

If you're thinking of becoming a comedian, there's a lot to consider. Telling funny jokes is only one ❶ _____ of the job. Presenting your material well is also important. So is finding an audience!

Being ❷ _____ funny is a gift. It isn't easy to be a comedian if being funny doesn't come to you naturally. Humor isn't really something you can learn, like spelling.

Many comedians borrow or adapt ideas from past comedians. There's nothing wrong with this. Comedians usually give

3 _____ to people whose work has influenced them.

When a joke falls flat, a quick recovery is important. Even if the comedian feels a lot of

4 _____, it shouldn't show. Sometimes it's easiest to simply say something like, "Wow, I can't believe I tried to get away with that rubbish!"

Remember this. An audience has a

5 _____ to laugh when they listen to a comedian. The audience wants to have fun. It isn't your enemy!

The Comedian

by D. J. Ortiz

"Do you know what the dinosaur said to the chicken?" Emilio asked.

The young children who were gathered around him looked shy. They also looked embarrassed. They were silent as stones. I felt some **tension** in the air. I'm Emilio's sister, and I know he wants to be a comedian.

"Oh, come on, take a guess!" he pleaded.

"What did the dinosaur say?" one little girl said.

"You look like dinner to me!" Emilio said. He laughed.

The three children simply stared at him. They began drifting away, heading for other parts of the playground.

"Did I say something wrong?" Emilio asked me.

I stared at his costume. His hair was covered with a black wig, and he wore a mustache, a big suit, and a tie. "I think I can answer your question," I told him.

Stop | Think | Write

SUMMARIZE

What is Emilio's problem?

_____

_____

_____

"Well?" Emilio said.

"Do you really want to become a comedian?"

"You know that I do. Too bad I can't even make a group of second graders laugh. I stink worse than a skunk convention," Emilio said.

"You're not that bad," I said. "I could give you some pointers—that is, if you'll listen to me."

"I'm listening, with all twelve ears."

"You don't have twelve ears," I said.

"Ha, ha, ha!" Emilio laughed. "I meant twelve years!"

"Stop right there," I said. "You have a **tendency** to laugh at your own jokes. Rule number one is no laughing at your own jokes."

"Why not?" asked Emilio, clearly puzzled.

I sighed and shook my head. "If the joke is funny, other people will laugh. No one will laugh just because you do."

Stop   Think   Write

VOCABULARY

What is Emilio's <u>tendency</u> after he tells a joke?

_____

_____

_____

"All right," Emilio said, "that's rule number one. What's rule number two?"

As patiently as possible, I said, "You have to start with the basics. You need to get your own material. Think of a theme or a story, and then use it to tell several jokes."

"What kind of theme do you mean?" he asked.

"Use your imagination," I replied. I suggested that he choose something ordinary, like dogs or baseball. I also said he could write about something as common as a watch or time. "The important thing," I said, "is to think up something that anyone can relate to."

Emilio seemed to be listening to me, and he went right to work. The next day he was ready with his new material. He said, "This new routine is going to make you laugh hysterically."

Stop Think Write

CAUSE AND EFFECT

Why is it important for a comedian to think of things that people can relate to?

_____

_____

_____

I waited patiently. I was ready to give him **credit** for his new material.

Emilio said, "Do you know the difference between a ship captain and a jeweler? The ship captain watches the sea, and the jeweler sees the watch. Do you know why the guy got rid of his watchdog? Because the dog couldn't tell time. The same guy threw his alarm clock out the window just to see time fly."

I just sat there without a trace of a smile on my face. I couldn't pretend his jokes were funny. If anything, I felt a bit annoyed. "I think those are the worst jokes I've ever heard," I said. "Did you really make those up?"

Emilio said, "I did what you said. I looked on the Internet. I found these jokes about a watch and a dog and telling time. You said I should do a theme."

"The best comedians don't use other people's jokes," I said. "They make them up!"

Stop | Think | Write

FACT AND OPINION

Emilio's sister says, "The best comedians don't use other people's jokes." Is this a fact or an opinion? Explain.

_____

_____

_____

"Oh, never mind," Emilio said. "I'm never going to be a comedian. I was no good at soccer. I can't spell very well. Let's face it, I'm the worst card in the pack."

I gave him a pat on the back. "No, you're not. I'm sure you will be successful. By the time I get through with you, you'll be the joker. You'll have people in stitches."

Emilio groaned, and I added, "What you need to do is make jokes about some **aspect** of your own life. You could tell about going to school or taking a family vacation. Or you could tell about the people you know. Think of your favorite comedians. They all make jokes about people they know."

"Okay, okay," Emilio said with more enthusiasm. "There's no lack of material in my life. I've got more material than a dress factory!"

"You're funnier when you don't try so hard," I said. "Get at it and write, big brother." To my surprise, he did.

Stop Think Write

VOCABULARY

What is an aspect of Emilio's life that he could write about?

_____

_____

_____

A few days later, Emilio had a routine ready. He tried out his new jokes on me. Maybe I didn't laugh, but I did smile. "Not bad," I said. "You have a few days to practice before my birthday party on Sunday."

"You think I'm ready for that?" he asked.

"The real question is, are we ready for you?" I said.

Everybody came on Sunday—aunts, uncles, grandparents, cousins. After dinner, I said, "I'd like to present Emilio, the Joker!" The family clapped politely.

Emilio cleared his throat. "I decided to become a comedian," he said, "because I'm not good at much else. I'm terrible at school. I was really happy that my last report card was terrible."

"Why were you happy?" I called out.

"Because at least Mom and Dad knew it was mine," Emilio said. Dad let out a guffaw, and I heard some laughter.

Stop | Think | Write

INFER AND PREDICT

Why does the family clap politely when Emilio's sister introduces him?

_____

_____

_____

Emilio said, "My parents think I should be like my relatives, but I'm not so sure. Take Uncle Luis. He makes those great pickles. Everyone loves them. So what? Why is a pickle such a big dill?" Uncle Luis let out a hoot.

Everyone laughed. "Good one," said Mom.

"I really wanted to be a good speller," Emilio said. "I tried everything. I wrote my spelling words over and over. I sang them in the shower. Finally, I swallowed a dictionary."

"How did it taste?" Uncle Luis asked.

"Educational," Emilio said. "My sister kept asking me if it helped, but I didn't say a thing. She wasn't getting a word out of me."

The family was **genuinely** impressed. Everyone clapped and laughed. Maybe there was hope for my brother after all.

Stop | **Think** | **Write**

Why is the family surprised by Emilio's act?

_____

_____

_____

Look Back and Respond

1 Who is Emilio's first audience in the story?

_____

_____

_____

Hint

For a clue, see page 44.

2 When Emilio's sister says, "You're funnier when you don't try so hard," is she stating a fact or an opinion? How can you tell?

_____

_____

_____

Hint

Remember, an opinion is what someone thinks or believes.

3 How has Emilio changed during the story?..

_____

_____

_____

Hint

Clues can be found on all pages.

4 How do people react to Emilio's jokes at the beginning of the story? How do they react to his jokes at the end of the story?

_____

_____

_____

Hint

For clues, see pages 44 and 50.

Lesson 6

✓ TARGET VOCABULARY

flair
fundamental
lingered
phenomenal
showdown

Early Radio Shows

Radio was a ① _____ invention that captured people's imaginations. Thousands of people wanted to experiment with this amazing new technology.

Until late 1912, there were no laws regulating radio transmitters in the United States. Anyone with a ② _____ for mechanical things could set up stations wherever they wished. These amateurs, known as "hams," were free to broadcast anything they wished, from wherever they happened to be.

In 1912, there was a **3** _____
between the radio operators and the government.
The government passed new rules setting limits on
who could transmit radio signals. This led to
4 _____ change in the way radio
shows were made.

In April of 1917, as the country entered World War I,
the U.S. government shut down all amateur stations
and took over the airwaves. Radio became a
device for communicating information. Families
5 _____ by the radio waiting
for news from the battlefields. It was not until
after the war that radio again became a source
of entertainment.

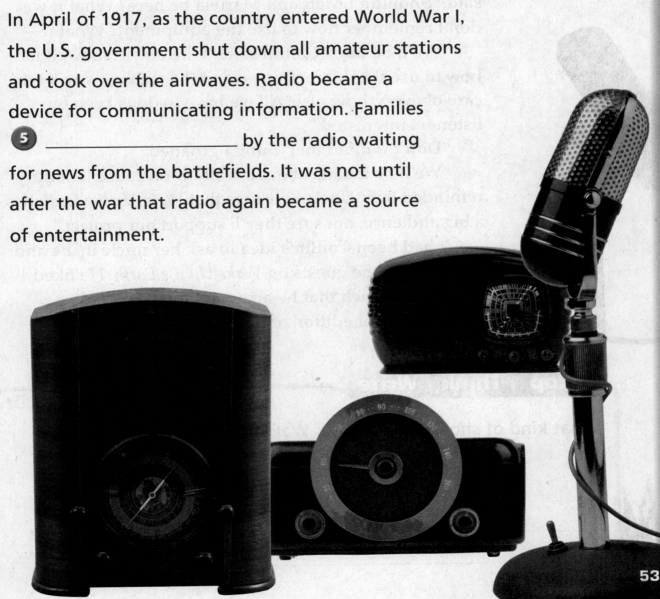

The Green Machine

by Dina McClellan

When Caitlin got to the WUHA radio station, Sunita was already there. She jumped up, her face filled with concern. "The show starts in just half an hour," Sunita said. "Shouldn't Matt and Mariela be here? What if we don't remember how to use the equipment? What if—"

"We'll be fine," Caitlin said. "Uncle Kyle showed us how to use the microphones, and the tech crew will take care of everything else. All we have to do is keep our listeners interested."

"Don't remind me!" Sunita groaned.

"We'll be talking about a really good cause," Caitlin reminded her. "Uncle Kyle says that *Wake Up the Earth* has a big audience. I'm sure they'll support our project."

It had been Caitlin's idea to ask her uncle if she and Sunita could be guests on *Wake Up the Earth*. He liked the idea so much that he arranged for them to do a special student edition of the show that they would host themselves.

Stop Think Write

CONCLUSIONS AND GENERALIZATIONS

What kind of show do you think *Wake Up the Earth* is?

_____

_____

_____

ON AIR

The girls didn't have any more time to worry. Mariela and Matt arrived, and before they knew it, the four of them were in the studio. Caitlin's uncle signaled to them from the booth. Then the ON AIR sign flashed red, and they were on.

"Good afternoon!" Sunita chirped nervously into the microphone. "I'm Sunita Tejani."

"And I'm Caitlin Ratliffe. We're here to host a special student edition of *Wake Up the Earth*."

"We have an awesome show for you today," Sunita said. "Our guests are Matt Reid and Mariela Guzman. They've formed new a group at our school, and they're planning amazing work."

Sunita was already sounding a little calmer. Caitlin smiled at her, and then said to Mariela and Matt, "Why don't you tell our listeners about what you're up to?"

Stop Think Write

CONCLUSIONS AND GENERALIZATIONS

Why do you think Sunita is nervous?

_____

_____

_____

"Matt and I started the Green Machine because we saw a **fundamental** problem at Greenwood Middle School and we wanted to do something about it," Mariela began.

"The school's appearance is pretty bad," Matt added. "The field is like a dust pit—there's almost no grass. There are holes in the fence, and the bushes in front of the school are dead because of some plant disease."

Sunita leaned forward and said into the microphone, "Why didn't the school do something about these problems?"

"Well, our teachers and principal are great," said Matt. "However, with recent cuts in the school budget, there's not a lot of money for extras like landscaping."

Mariela had a photograph of the school with her. She put it on the table and said, "The school grounds have gotten so bad that some kids started leaving trash around."

Stop · Think · Write

MAIN IDEAS AND DETAILS

What basic problem do Matt and Mariela want to solve at their school?

_____

_____

_____

"What can the Green Machine do to make things better?" Caitlin asked.

"For starters, we'd like to fix the fence, plant new grass, and get some new bushes to replace the dead ones," Matt explained. "Then maybe kids will stop littering."

Caitlin took a deep breath. Matt had just given her the cue to make her pitch for help. "I'm sure there must be people in our audience who can support the Green Machine," she said. "Listeners, if you have some extra grass seed, the Green Machine could use it!"

Sunita chimed in with requests for donations to mend the school's fence and plant new bushes. Then, after thanking their guests, Sunita and Caitlin ended the show.

"You two really have a **flair** for radio!" Matt said.

Sunita and Caitlin grinned at each other. "Now comes the hard part," said Caitlin. "Waiting to see what kind of response we get!"

Stop | Think | Write

STORY STRUCTURE

What problem does the Green Machine have?

_____

_____

_____

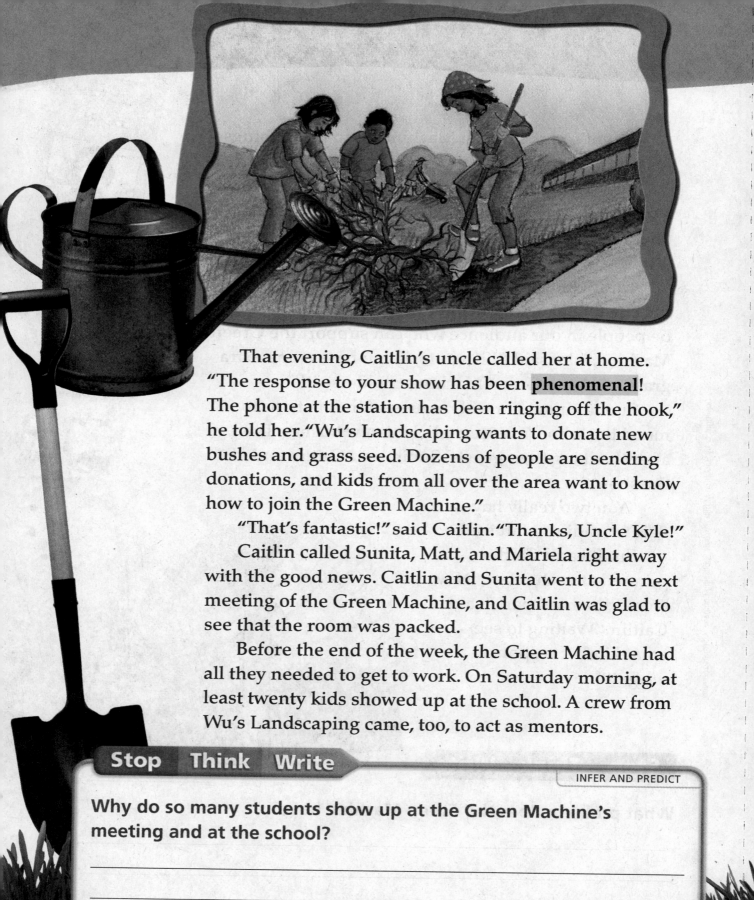

That evening, Caitlin's uncle called her at home. "The response to your show has been **phenomenal!** The phone at the station has been ringing off the hook," he told her. "Wu's Landscaping wants to donate new bushes and grass seed. Dozens of people are sending donations, and kids from all over the area want to know how to join the Green Machine."

"That's fantastic!" said Caitlin. "Thanks, Uncle Kyle!"

Caitlin called Sunita, Matt, and Mariela right away with the good news. Caitlin and Sunita went to the next meeting of the Green Machine, and Caitlin was glad to see that the room was packed.

Before the end of the week, the Green Machine had all they needed to get to work. On Saturday morning, at least twenty kids showed up at the school. A crew from Wu's Landscaping came, too, to act as mentors.

Stop Think Write

INFER AND PREDICT

Why do so many students show up at the Green Machine's meeting and at the school?

_____

_____

_____

Caitlin could hardly believe how much they accomplished in a single day. One crew went around with garbage bags and cleaned up trash. Mr. Wu directed a second group as they dug up dead bushes and planted new ones. His son showed a third group of students how to sprinkle grass seeds.

"This field will be covered with lush, green grass before you know it," said Mr. Wu.

Caitlin felt proud when the principal came by to thank them for all their hard work. Everyone clapped when he put up a sign that read, "This project completed by THE GREEN MACHINE." Caitlin, Sunita, Mariela, and Matt **lingered** at the school after the others left. They were amazed by how different—and how much nicer—their school looked now.

Stop | Think | Write

VOCABULARY

Why might Caitlin, Sunita, Mariela, and Matt have <u>lingered</u> at the school?

_____

_____

_____

A week later, Caitlin, Sunita, Matt, and Mariela were back on the air at WUHA.

"Before we begin this week's episode of *Wake Up the Earth*, we want to thank our listeners for their response to last week's show," Sunita said into the microphone.

The four students briefly talked about the donations they had received and the work the Green Machine had done at the school. Then Caitlin asked, "What's next for the Green Machine?"

"We're getting ready for a **showdown** with town officials," Matt said. "The town closed a local playground, but we think it should be fixed up and reopened. Kids in the neighborhood need a place to play."

Sunita looked at the photograph that Mariela held up. "You've got your work cut out for you," Sunita said. "However, if anyone can do it, the Green Machine can."

Stop | Think | Write

VOCABULARY

What might happen during a <u>showdown</u> between the Green Machine and town officials?

_____

_____

_____

Look Back and Respond

1 Do you think that WUHA is a large or a small radio station? Explain.

_____

_____

_____

Hint

For clues, see pages 54, 55, and 58.

2 How does Caitlin try to make Sunita feel less nervous?

_____

_____

_____

Hint

For clues, see pages 54 and 55.

3 Why might someone go on the radio to get support for a cause?

_____

_____

_____

Hint

Think about how many people might listen to the radio.

4 What do you think will be the result of the showdown between the Green Machine and town officials? Explain.

_____

_____

_____

Hint

Think about how well the Green Machine's plan to fix up the school worked.

Lesson 7

✓ TARGET VOCABULARY

customary
initially
intense
multitude
originated

The Maya

1 The Maya once inhabited as many as forty large cities. A **multitude** of people lived in each city. The population of some Mayan cities reached 50,000 people. At one time, there were as many as two million Maya altogether.

Name something other than people that might exist in a <u>multitude</u>.

_____

_____

_____

2 It was **customary** for Mayan cities to contain temples, palaces, and pyramids. Every Mayan city also usually had a central square and a court for playing ball.

What is your <u>customary</u> way to dress for school?

_____

_____

_____

3 The Maya had a system of writing that used symbols. In the 1830s, people began to study Mayan writing. **Initially**, the symbols were puzzling. Eventually, people learned the meanings of the symbols.

Tell about something that was initially difficult but that you eventually learned to do well.

_____

_____

_____

4 The Mayan people sometimes fought one another. **Intense** conflicts arose between Maya who lived in different cities. Fighting was sometimes brutal and caused many deaths.

Describe an intense rivalry between two sports teams that you know of.

_____

_____

_____

5 The Mayan civilization **originated** over 3,500 years ago. The Maya flourished until about 1,000 years ago. No one is sure why the Mayan civilization declined. There are no written records of what happened.

What is a synonym of originated?

_____

The Mighty Maya

by Claire Daniel

Victor's teacher was talking about the Mayan civilization, which had dominated Mexico's Yucatán peninsula long ago. **Initially**, Victor was not interested. He had been to the Yucatán to visit his grandparents. Ruins of a Mayan city were near their home. Victor didn't understand why people would want to see crumbling old stones.

Then his teacher began talking about Gonzalo Guerrero, a Spanish explorer who had loved the Maya. Victor perked up. His last name was Guerrero, too! Was Gonzalo Guerrero his ancestor? That evening, Victor asked his father, but he didn't know.

The next day, Victor's teacher asked his students to choose a topic for a report. Victor chose to write about the Maya. His father gave him a book to read. This is what Victor learned.

Stop Think Write

CAUSE AND EFFECT

Why did Victor suddenly become more interested in the Maya?

_____

_____

_____

Mayan Civilization

The Mayan culture **originated** as far back as 3,700 years ago. The Maya lived in what is now Mexico and Central America. They developed a great civilization. They understood many mathematical and scientific concepts. They knew a lot about how the sun and moon moved in the sky. The Maya used a calendar with 365 days before Europeans did.

The Maya built things based on nature. They built large pyramids to look like mountains. In the Mayan city of Chichén Itzá, one temple in the shape of a pyramid still stands. The Maya built the temple so that the number of its steps matched the number of days in a year. Each of the temple's four sides has 91 steps. There are 364 steps in all, and the top of the pyramid is step number 365.

The Maya built roads between their great cities. The roads were white so that they looked like the Milky Way in the sky. The Maya used the roads to trade goods and travel to important temples. The white roads led to the center of each Mayan city.

Chichén Itzá

Stop | Think | Write

VOCABULARY

Describe when and where the Mayan culture originated.

_____

_____

_____

Daily Life and Work

Each member of a Mayan family helped with daily chores. Mayan men worked in the fields. They fished and hunted and gathered fruits and vegetables. It was **customary** for women to take care of the house and tend to the animals. Women also made blankets, clothes, pottery, and baskets.

Trading was an important part of Mayan culture. The Maya traded jewelry, jade, feathers, and cloth for food and other items. Some Maya also had cotton, wax, honey, and salt to trade. Mayan traders went to Honduras to trade for cocoa. They used cocoa seeds to make chocolate.

Mayan traders traveled in large canoes that looked like floating wagons. Each boat could hold twenty-five people and a large load of goods to trade. The Maya used maps written on cotton cloth to guide them.

When the Maya traveled, they met new people. They learned about new ideas and different cultures.

Stop · Think · Write

VOCABULARY

What were three tasks that were <u>customary</u> for Mayan women to do?

_____

_____

_____

Spanish Explorers

In 1492, the explorer Christopher Columbus arrived in America. He called the land the New World. Columbus led the exploration for Spain. After hearing of his trip, other Spanish explorers traveled to the New World. Some found great riches. They took gold and silver that they found.

Sailors told stories. They described the New World. Many people who heard the stories wanted to see the beautiful new land for themselves. Some wanted gold and silver. Others wanted adventure.

In 1511, a Spanish ship sank near the Yucatán. Twenty sailors clung to a lifeboat. They floated for two weeks. The weather was **intense**, with severe storms and winds. The sailors had few supplies and little food or water.

Only two men survived. One was named Jerónimo de Aguilar. The other man was Gonzalo Guerrero.

Stop Think Write

CAUSE AND EFFECT

Why did so many Spanish people want to come to America?

_____

_____

_____

Guerrero and the Maya

The two men drifted ashore on the Yucatán coast. They landed in the center of the Mayan civilization.

At that time, Spain had not yet conquered Mexico. The Maya captured Guerrero and Aguilar and made them work as slaves. The Mayan chief liked Guerrero. The chief's daughter even fell in love with him. Guerrero married the princess and was a slave no more. He became part of the royal family and a leader of the army.

Guerrero loved his life with the Maya. However, he knew that more Spanish would come. The Spanish had attacked native peoples in other parts of America. Guerrero knew that they would attack the Maya and take their riches. He warned the Maya that strange men would arrive. He taught the Maya how to defend their land and their goods.

Stop Think Write

MAIN IDEAS AND DETAILS

How did Guerrero know that Spanish soldiers would one day come to the Yucatán?

_____

_____

_____

Spanish soldiers did arrive. In 1519, Hernando Cortés came to the Yucatán. He heard about the two Spanish men who lived with the Maya. Cortés sent for them. Aguilar came quickly. Cortés asked Aguilar to join his army, and Aguilar agreed.

Cortés went to see Guerrero. He was dressed as a Maya. Cortés asked Guerrero to join his soldiers, but Guerrero said no. He told Cortés that he was happy with the Maya. Cortés left without Guerrero.

Another Spanish conqueror, Francisco Montejo, also asked Guerrero to join his army. Once again, Guerrero refused. Montejo led a **multitude** of soldiers against the Maya. The Maya fought bravely, with Guerrero as their leader. Guerrero probably died in one of the battles.

Francisco Montejo never did conquer the Maya. Many people believe it was because of Gonzalo Guerrero. They are grateful for what he did to help the Maya.

Stop Think Write

PERSUASION

How does the author want readers to feel about Guerrero? How can you tell?

_____

_____

_____

Victor closed the book. He asked his father what had happened to the Mayan civilization.

"People left the Mayan cities, but no one knows why," his father said. "However, there are Mayan ruins in Mexico that we can visit."

"Like Chichén Itzá?" asked Victor.

"That's right," his father said. "About 800 years ago, many Maya left Chichén Itzá. They might have left because there wasn't enough to eat. It's also possible that a disease killed everyone."

"Can we visit Grandpa and Grandma soon?" Victor asked. "I want to go to Chichén Itzá. I want to find out why Guerrero loved the Maya so much. If we visit the ruins, maybe I can find clues."

His dad grinned. "You don't still think the Mayan ruins are just a bunch of crumbling stones?" he asked.

"They're more than just stones. They're what's left of a great civilization," said Victor.

Stop **Think** **Write**

INFER AND PREDICT

How can ruins of Mayan cities give clues to what Mayan civilization was like?

_____

_____

_____

Look Back and Respond

1 How do Victor's feelings about the Maya change from the beginning of the story to the end?

_____

_____

_____

Hint

For clues, look on pages 64 and 70.

2 Name two facts that the author uses to try to persuade readers that the Maya had a great civilization.

_____

_____

_____

Hint

For clues, look on page 65.

3 Do you think that the author admires Gonzalo Guerrero? How can you tell?

_____

_____

_____

Hint

For clues, look on pages 68 and 69.

4 Do you think the author wants readers to think that visiting Mayan ruins would be informative and interesting? Explain.

_____

_____

_____

Hint

For clues, look on page 70.

complex
elegant
principle
reluctant
specimens

School Science Fairs

Check the answer.

1 A display in a science fair might demonstrate a scientific _____.

☐ **mentor**   ☐ **principle**   ☐ **elegant**

2 Sometimes a simple display may beat a more _____ display.

☐ **reluctant**   ☐ **literary**   ☐ **complex**

3 Display all the _____ that you have gathered for your display.

☐ **transmissions**   ☐ **specimens**   ☐ **principle**

4 Try to find an _____ way to explain a complicated idea.

☐ **elegant**   ☐ **aspect**   ☐ **reluctant**

5 Don't be _____ to try something new!

☐ **brainwashed**   ☐ **elegant**   ☐ **reluctant**

6 What is the most <u>complex</u> task that you do every day? Explain.

_____

_____

_____

7 What chores are you <u>reluctant</u> to do? Explain.

_____

_____

_____

8 Name a <u>principle</u> that you think a politician should follow.

_____

_____

_____

A Prize to DYE For!

by Shirley Granahan

Hi, I'm Josie, and I love being a winner. Lucky for me, I'm the fastest runner on my block. I know that to be the best, you have to train and keep in shape. So I practice every day. I definitely don't like to lose!

Not to brag or anything, but I'm also the best speller in school. I won the spelling bee last year. I'm the best at math and science, too. It takes hard work to be the best, so I spend a lot of time alone, studying.

Once a year, however, I'm pretty popular. Our school has a science fair. All the kids want to be my partner so they'll win. Even though I have a partner, I usually end up doing most of the work myself! This year, I decided things were going to be different.

Stop Think Write

CAUSE AND EFFECT

Why is Josie popular once a year?

_____

_____

_____

I thought of an **elegant** solution to my problem: I would ask Max to be my partner. He's the second smartest kid in class, even though he clowns around a lot. If we did the project together, I knew we would win, and we wouldn't have to compete with each other!

This morning, our teacher announced the date of this year's fair. Right after lunch, I went up to Max. "Would you be my science fair partner?" I asked.

Max looked surprised. "Why me?" he asked.

"Together we can plan a great project," I said. "Neither of us will end up doing all the work!"

"I hear you!" Max said. He knew all about picking a partner who didn't help much. "It's a deal!" he said. "Together we'll create an amazing winning project!"

Stop **Think** **Write**

SEQUENCE OF EVENTS

What does Josie do right after lunch?

_____

_____

_____

Max is into space stuff, so he suggested we do something about stars. "The bright city lights make it hard to see the stars!" I reminded him.

I suggested we make a volcano and measure lava flow. "No way," Max said. "That would be too **complex** and too expensive. We'd need to make volcano models and find a way to simulate lava. We'd have to run hundreds of tests, as well."

Max looked thoughtful. "Let's test which plants make the best natural dyes . . . it would be a project to DYE for!" he laughed.

"Good idea!" I said, glad that I'd picked Max. He was silly sometimes, but he had great ideas. "All we need are plants, a pot, and something to dye!"

The next day, my mom took us shopping. At the market, we bought carrots, lettuce, celery, blueberries, and beets. At a fabric shop, we found white cotton on sale. "We can use this to test the dyes," Max said.

INFER AND PREDICT

Where do Josie and Max live? How do you know?

_____

_____

_____

We spent the next week doing research. We read the basic **principle** for making dyes. Mostly, it's boiling the plants in water. "I like to cook," I said. "Why don't I be in charge of making the dyes? You can be in charge of dyeing the cloth."

Max agreed. So I tested how long to cook the fruits and vegetables, and at what temperatures.

On Saturday, Max came over. I cooked the carrots, then Max dipped in the cloth. The carrots didn't really color the fabric. We took photos to show our process and also what didn't work.

Next, we tried lettuce and celery, but they were no good either. Then we did blueberries. They were great! The cotton turned blue. Then we tried beets. Great! The cotton turned a bright pinkish red.

Stop | **Think** | **Write**

What other word could the author have used that means the same as principle?

_____

_____

_____

We needed to try one more plant, and Max suggested bright green leaves from one of Mom's plants. She carefully cut off a few leaves for us. After a few hours of cooking them, I'd made yellow dye!

The next day, Max said, "You know, we should dye things more interesting than bits of cotton!"

I thought that was a great idea. Max donated a white shirt, and we decided it should be dyed blue. The only white thing I had was my stuffed bear. "That bear would look awesome in yellow!" Max said.

At first, I was **reluctant**, but finally I agreed. "So, now what should we make bright red?" I asked.

"I've got a great idea for that," Max said with a smile. "Don't worry. It'll be great. You'll see it at the fair."

Stop | Think | Write

SEQUENCE OF EVENTS

What color dye does Josie make last? What does she use to make it?

_____

_____

_____

On the day of the fair, we set up our display. It was a warm day, but Max was wearing his winter hat. "I overslept and my hair is a mess," he explained.

We hung a sign over our display: WHICH PLANTS DYE BEST? We put up photos of our process. We had the bits of cotton with no results from carrots, lettuce, and celery. We had the colored cotton bits, too. We placed the **specimens** under their pictures. Finally, we put out the real things we'd dyed. Max's shirt was a perfect blue and my bear had lovely yellow fur. Still, it was obvious that something was missing!

"Where's whatever you dyed red ?" I asked.

"You'll see it soon enough," Max laughed.

"I take competitions seriously, Max," I said.

"So do I, Josie" he replied. "You have to learn to relax and have a little fun!"

Just then, the judges came to our display.

Stop Think Write

VOCABULARY

What are the specimens that Max and Josie place in their display?

_____

_____

_____

PLANTS DYE BEST?

"Why is there no red item?" asked one judge. "Your report indicates that you used beets."

"We did," I replied. I stared at Max, waiting for him to answer the judge.

Suddenly, Max ripped off his hat. He had bright red hair! "Ta-da!" he sang. "I've been DYEING to show off my hair all day!"

All the judges laughed. I laughed, too. Max may have done things differently, but he made our project special. He also taught me to have more fun!

Thanks to Max, winning was a lot more fun this year! (We won first prize, of course.)

Stop | Think | Write

CAUSE AND EFFECT

Why do the judges laugh?

_____

_____

_____

Look Back and Respond

1 Why does Josie ask Max to be her partner?

_____

_____

_____

Hint

For a clue, see page 75.

2 Which kind of plant do Josie and Max test first?

_____

_____

_____

Hint

For a clue, see page 77.

3 Why do you think Josie is reluctant to dye her bear?

_____

_____

_____

Hint

Think about something you've owned for a long time.

4 How does working together on the project help both Josie and Max?

_____

_____

_____

Hint

Think about how they work together.

defy
permeated
rudimentary
sparsely
venture

WORLD WAR II
in the Pacific

During World War II, many battles were fought on islands in the Pacific Ocean. Japanese soldiers controlled many of the islands. The United States and its allies had to defeat the Japanese in the Pacific if they hoped to win the war.

A culture of pride and obedience **permeated** the Japanese army. The Japanese were disciplined fighters. Most would never **defy** their commanders. They were trained to carry out orders without question. They would not stop fighting without an order to do so. This made the Japanese a very fierce enemy.

Many of the islands in the Pacific were **sparsely** populated. There were often no roads and no towns. Living conditions were **rudimentary**, with just basic shelter and simple food. Japanese soldiers often hid in the dense jungle. American soldiers had to **venture** into the jungle to look for the enemy. Capturing each island was a difficult challenge for the Americans and their allies.

1 Living conditions on many of the islands in the Pacific were _____.

2 A sense of pride and obedience _____ the Japanese army from top to bottom.

3 Most Japanese soldiers obeyed orders and would never _____ a commanding officer.

4 The U.S. army often had to _____ into the dense jungle to find and fight the enemy.

5 Many of the islands in the Pacific were _____ populated and had just a few communities of farmers and fishermen.

6 If we say that an area is <u>sparsely</u> populated, what do we mean?

_____

_____

_____

7 What do you think would happen to a soldier if he or she chose to <u>defy</u> an officer's order?

_____

_____

_____

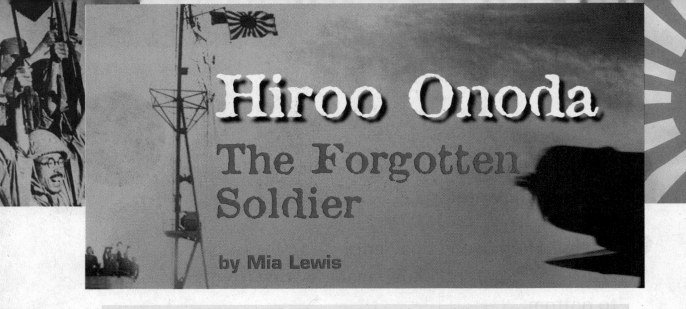

Hiroo Onoda
The Forgotten Soldier

by Mia Lewis

Imagine that you are outside at lunchtime and don't hear the bell. Once you see that everyone else has gone inside, you'd run back to class, wouldn't you?

However, what if you thought all your friends were still outside? What if you thought they were hiding, trying to *trick* you into thinking lunch was over? Would you stay outside just to **defy** them and prove their trick wouldn't work? Would you stay outside for, say, an entire week? Probably not.

In a way, that is what happened to Hiroo Onoda. He was a Japanese army intelligence officer during World War II. In 1944, Onoda was sent to Lubang Island, in the Philippines. World War II was raging in the Philippines and on other Pacific islands. The war ended in 1945, but Hiroo Onoda didn't know that. He stayed on the island until he finally surrendered, thirty years later.

Stop | Think | Write

CAUSE AND EFFECT

Why did Hiroo Onoda go to Lubang Island in 1944?

_____

_____

_____

Following Orders

When Onoda arrived on Lubang Island, it was controlled by the Japanese. Onoda's task was to do everything in his power to stop American forces from taking over the island. Even if he could not stop them, Onoda was to fight the Americans any way he could. He was ordered to keep fighting until his Japanese commander came back for him.

Onoda took his orders very seriously. Soon after he arrived on Lubang Island, American forces took control of it. Japanese soldiers retreated into the jungle and hid in this **sparsely** inhabited area. The soldiers separated into small groups so they would be harder to find. American soldiers captured or killed most of the Japanese soldiers on the island. Before long, Onoda and three other men were the only Japanese soldiers left in hiding.

| Stop | Think | Write | VOCABULARY |

Why do you think the jungle was <u>sparsely</u> inhabited?

_____

_____

_____

85

The War Ends—Or Does It?

Onoda and the three other soldiers lived on the few supplies they had taken with them into the jungle. They ate bananas and coconuts. Sometimes they killed local farm animals for food. With no real shelter or extra clothes, the Japanese men lived a **rudimentary** life.

Sometimes the soldiers would **venture** out to fight the enemy. The Japanese thought the Americans were still the enemy, but they also suspected local residents. Onoda thought that locals might be spies, or enemy troops in disguise. Sometimes the Japanese attacked locals, killed their animals, or burned their crops.

World War II ended in August of 1945. In October, Onoda saw leaflets that said the war was over and that soldiers should come out of hiding. Onoda did not trust the leaflets. He thought they were a trick. He decided to stay well hidden and follow the orders his commander had given him.

Stop Think Write

CAUSE AND EFFECT

Why did the Japanese soldiers attack local people?

_____

_____

_____

Soldiering On

Year after year, Onoda and his men hid in the jungle. In 1949, one of the soldiers in Onoda's group couldn't take living in isolation any longer. He wanted to surrender. He didn't tell the others. He simply left. He made his way out of the jungle and surrendered to the authorities in Lubang.

Onoda worried that the deserter might tell the enemy where they were hiding. He and the two other Japanese men became more careful than ever. They continued to suspect local people of working with the enemy. They carried out more attacks. Lubang officials sent army patrols to fight back. This led to some small battles between Onoda and local troops.

To Onoda, these battles proved the war was still going on. How could it be over when the enemy was still attacking them? Another of Onoda's men was killed in a battle in 1954. Now, just Onoda and one other man remained.

Stop **Think** **Write**

CAUSE AND EFFECT

Why was Onoda convinced that the war was not over?

_____

_____

_____

Come Out, Come Out!

While Hiroo Onoda and his men were in hiding, people tried unsuccessfully to persuade them that the war was over. A great many leaflets were dropped from planes or placed where Japanese soldiers might find them. A surrender order from a Japanese general was printed on one of the leaflets. Newspapers announcing the end of the war were left. Notes and photographs from relatives and friends were dropped from planes. Friends and relatives spoke out over loudspeakers.

Onoda and his men carefully read all the leaflets. They considered every piece of material they found. They always found something suspicious and concluded that the leaflets were a clever trick. They had been at war in the jungle for so long that suspicion **permeated** their lives. They found it very difficult to trust anyone or anything.

Stop Think Write

What evidence shows that suspicion __permeated__ the lives of Onoda and his men?

_____

_____

_____

The Search for Onoda

Onoda's final companion died in a battle with locals in 1972. He was fifty-one years old, and he had been hiding for twenty-seven years. Onoda was the only remaining Japanese soldier. Even so, he continued to carry out his commander's orders.

By this time, Hiroo Onoda was something of a legend in Japan. Many people had heard of him. In 1974, a young man named Norio Suzuki left Japan for a trip to the Philippines, Burma, Nepal, and other countries. He said he was going to look for Hiroo Onoda. Amazingly, after just a few days on Lubang, Suzuki found Onoda!

Suzuki told Onoda that World War II was over, but Onoda did not believe him. He said that he would take orders only from his commander. Suzuki took photographs of Onoda. The two men agreed on a hiding place for messages. Then Suzuki went back to Japan. He wanted to help bring Onoda home.

| Stop | Think | Write |

INFER AND PREDICT

Why do you think Norio Suzuki took pictures of Onoda?

_____

_____

_____

Out of the Jungle

Norio Suzuki showed the photographs of Onoda to Japanese officials. The government located Major Taniguchi, Onoda's commander from thirty years earlier. Taniguchi now sold books for a living. He agreed to help.

Suzuki left a message for Onoda at their agreed hiding place. He also left copies of the photographs he had taken. Onoda had not seen himself during the entire time he had been hiding in the jungle. He was struck by how much his face had changed.

On March 9, 1974, Major Taniguchi arrived and gave Onoda the order to stop fighting. At long last, Onoda had acceptable proof that the war was over. He handed over his gun and surrendered.

After almost thirty years in hiding, Hiroo Onoda came out of the jungle. He went back to Japan where he received a hero's welcome.

Stop **Think** **Write**

CAUSE AND EFFECT

Why did Major Taniguchi have to travel to Lugang to speak to Onoda in person?

_____

_____

_____

Look Back and Respond

1 **Why did Onoda continue to fight for so long?**

_____

_____

_____

Hint

For clues, look on pages 85, 88, and 89.

2 **Why did one of Onoda's men disobey orders and leave the jungle?**

_____

_____

_____

Hint

For clues, look on page 87.

3 **Why didn't Onoda and his men believe the leaflets they found?**

_____

_____

_____

Hint

For clues, look on page 88.

4 **What might have happened if Major Taniguchi had not gone to Lubang Island in 1974?**

_____

_____

_____

Hint

Think about what Onoda required before he would stop fighting.

✓ TARGET VOCABULARY

abundance
cultural
heritage
lore
retains

The Inuit

In the Arctic tundra, where Inuit communities are located, building materials are scarce. However, there is an **1** _____ of snow. In the past, the Inuit made temporary homes called igloos from hard-packed snow cut into blocks. The domed shape of the igloos helped to hold the heat. Each igloo had a skylight made of freshwater ice. When summer arrived, the igloos melted and the Inuit families moved into tents made of animal skins.

Although Inuit life has changed dramatically over the last century, the Inuit people continue to treasure many of their traditions. Inuit storytelling, mythology, and **2** _____ remain an important part of the **3** _____ life of the Inuit people.

Drumming is an important part of the Inuit ④ _____, too. Drums were traditionally made from driftwood and caribou skin, covered with walrus or seal skin. Drum dancing is used in ceremonies such as marriages, births, and a boy's coming-of-age.

Inuit culture ⑤ _____ a sense of a shared past and an understanding that the world around them is changing. Although the Inuit hunt and fish using state-of-the-art equipment, they also use age-old techniques that have been passed down through the generations.

Good Luck, Aputik!

by Dina McClellan

It's winter in the Arctic. In the tiny Inuit village where Nanuq and his family live, it is dark most of the time. The sun peeks out for only a few hours each day. For much of the day, the only light is a faint blue sheen the Moon casts over the icy snow.

Nanuq means "polar bear" in the Inuit language, and it suits the boy. He doesn't mind the cold. After the evening meal, he runs out to the wooded area behind his house and follows the familiar trail to the river. He darts through the trees, graceful as a gazelle, careful not to slip on the snow and ice. The river is frozen solid and as smooth as glass. Nanuq sits by the river's edge, breathing in the fresh, clean, northern air. He's waiting, listening. He hears only silence and the howling of the wind.

Stop Think Write

COMPARE AND CONTRAST

How is Nanuq like a polar bear?

_____

_____

_____

Before long, Nanuq hears what he's been waiting for: the sh-shush of a dogsled and the soft jingling of bells on the dog collars. It's Aputik's sled coming around the bend!

Nanuq knows that his uncle Aputik is practicing for the Iditarod that will take place the following week. The Iditarod is a race for mushers, who are dogsled racers, and their dog-pulled sleds. The Iditarod starts in southern Alaska and ends 1,100 miles to the northwest. It is very difficult, and only the best mushers compete.

Nanuq wants to be a musher like his uncle, but for now he is content to watch and cheer Aputik from a distance. "Go, Aputik!" Nanuq shouts, jumping up and down and waving his arms. His uncle doesn't hear him. Nanuq watches his sled glide across the snow. Then it vanishes into the dark night as swiftly as it appeared.

Stop | Think | Write

INFER AND PREDICT

Why do you think Nanuq is not a musher like his uncle?

_____

_____

_____

There is excitement in the village when Nanuq returns. A big celebration in Aputik's honor is about to take place in the snowhouse. People have come from all over by snowmobile and dogsled. There will be drumming, dancing, and singing to wish Aputik good luck. There will also be an **abundance** of food for everyone to eat.

The Inuit have a special way to play drums for dancing and singing. Drumming is part of their **heritage**, and Nanuq's father is an expert. The drum he has brought to the snowhouse used to belong to his father. The drum is large, flat, and round. He plays it by tapping the rim—not the head—on each side. He taps in a steady rhythm that starts out slow and gradually gets faster.

Nanuq's father sways back and forth as he drums. The women of the village, including Nanuq's mother and grandmother, gather around him and sway, too.

Stop Think Write

Write a detail from the text that shows that drumming is part of the <u>heritage</u> of Nanuq's father.

_____

_____

_____

96

The women sing in a special way called "throat singing." They make sounds deep in their throats. Sometimes the sounds imitate the calls of wolves, foxes, birds, and walruses. Sometimes they are words that tell of real-life experiences. Singing is one way of passing on the tribe's **lore** from generation to generation.

Tonight the women sing about a team of sled dogs and a brave musher. Their song describes how the musher races for his village and how well he treats his dogs. There is also a young boy in the song who stands by the musher—even on cold, lonely runs by the river.

Everyone understands that the musher in the song is Aputik and that the young boy is Nanuq. Nanuq cannot stop himself from grinning with pleasure. He is proud of his uncle. He is proud of his father, too, because his drumming keeps the rhythm for everyone else.

Stop | Think | Write

COMPARE AND CONTRAST

Write two ways in which the women's song imitates real life.

_____

_____

_____

As the women sing, they form a circle and start to dance. Dancing is a big part of the **cultural** life of the Inuits. No two dances are exactly alike. Like the songs, they are created especially for the occasion. Aputik leaps into the circle and starts stamping the ground to the steady beat of the drums. He whirls and twirls and stomps his feet, never failing to keep the beat. Nanuq is impressed by his uncle's fancy footwork.

The drum dancing and singing go on for hours. Even though it's −30°F (−34.4°C) outside, the snowhouse **retains** warmth. Inside, it is warm and cozy, and the yellow light of a dozen lanterns throws shadows on the walls. Nanuq's father taps faster on the sides of the drum, and the pace of the dance quickens. Then the song ends and the drumming fades out. All Nanuq can hear is the whooshing of the wind outside.

Stop   Think   Write

Why is it important that the snowhouse <u>retains</u> warmth?

_____

_____

_____

Suddenly, the silence is broken by wild cheering and the stomping of feet. The people hoot, holler, whoop, yelp, and make animal noises. Cries of "Good luck! Good luck!" can be heard. The women gather around Aputik, clucking and cooing over him, while the men entertain each other with racing lore of the past. Nanuq and his mother squeeze through the crowd to speak to Aputik.

"The song was a special gift for you," says Nanuq's mother. "Carry it in your heart. It will guide you on your journey and keep you safe."

Nanuq looks sad. "I won't be there to cheer you on," he tells his uncle.

The musher smiles and ruffles the boy's hair. "No," he says, "but you will be in my heart. You are a part of my song, and that will bring me good luck."

Nanuq looks into Aputik's dark, shining eyes and knows that what his uncle says is true. Nanuq feels certain that his uncle will win the race, like the brave musher in the song.

Stop Think Write

COMPARE AND CONTRAST

According to Nanuq, in what way is Aputik like the musher in the song?

_____

_____

_____

The Iditarod:

The Greatest Race on Earth

* The Iditarod is run on a trail that was originally a mail-supply route.

* The race begins in Anchorage, Alaska. It ends in Nome, Alaska.

* Teams of mushers and dogs complete the race in about 9 to17 days.

* In 1925, the trail was turned into a lifesaving highway for the children of Nome, Alaska, who were suffering from a deadly disease.

* Unless medicine was delivered, the sick children would die. Teams of mushers and dogs successfully transported the medicine.

* The Iditarod is a tribute to the mushers and dog teams that saved the children of Nome.

* Although sled dogs have been used for thousands of years, the first Iditarod took place in 1973. Thirty-five mushers competed in the race.

* The winner of the first Iditarod completed the race in twenty days. In 2008, the winner finished in just over nine days.

Stop | Think | Write

COMPARE AND CONTRAST

How has the Iditarod changed between 1973 and today?

_____

_____

_____

Look Back and Respond

1 How is the Arctic climate the same or different from the climate where you live?

_____

_____

_____

Hint

Compare the setting on page 94 to the climate where you live.

2 Name three things the villagers at the celebration do to honor Aputik.

_____

_____

_____

Hint

For clues, look on pages 96, 97, and 99.

3 How does Nanuq feel about his uncle?

_____

_____

_____

Hint

For clues, look on pages 95, 97, 98, and 99.

4 How does the celebration in the story compare with celebrations that you know?

_____

_____

_____

Hint

Reread the text. Think about celebrations you have attended.

✓ TARGET VOCABULARY

eerie
frothing
jutted
mounting
stabilize

Dangers at Sea

Piloting a boat at sea can be dangerous and scary. Fog can make it difficult to see what's ahead. Rocks or other ships may appear **eerie** and ghostlike in the mist.

Storms can stir up **mounting** waves and churning, rough waters. When you see the white foam of **frothing** waves, you know that the waves are very powerful. A sea captain has to **stabilize** the ship in rough waters so that it doesn't tip over.

In the nineteenth century, sea captains didn't have radios or radar to help them navigate. They relied on the beams of a lighthouse to warn them of dangers near shore. They had to be careful not to crash into sharp rocks that **jutted** out of the water.

1 A ship can tip over in rough seas if the captain does not _____ it.

2 You can see white foam on the tops of waves that are _____.

3 Fog can make ships or rocks look

_____.

4 Some effects of storms are rough waters and _____ waves.

5 Ships could be damaged if they crashed into rocks that _____ out of the water.

6 How would you feel if you saw an <u>eerie</u> shape through the mist?

_____

_____

_____

7 If we say that waves are <u>mounting</u>, what do we mean?

_____

_____

Grace to the Rescue

by Margaret Maugenest

Grace Darling grew up in an English lighthouse during the early nineteenth century. This is her story.

My family lived all alone on a tiny island surrounded by the sea. It was just the four of us: Mum, Dad, my younger brother, Willie, and me. We lived in the island's 75-foot tall lighthouse.

The nearby waters were very dangerous. Jagged rocks **jutted** above the waves. More rocks hid just beneath the surface, waiting to rip apart passing ships. Many ships had sunk in our waters. People spoke of ghosts that swam in the waves.

Our family seldom had visitors. Why would anyone come to this quiet, lonely place? Sometimes I longed for adventure, but life on our island was quiet and simple. Keeping the lighthouse lamp burning was our most important task. My father conducted his work seriously. He knew how sea captains depended upon him.

Stop | Think | Write

UNDERSTANDING CHARACTERS

How does Grace feel about her life on the island?

_____

_____

_____

The night that changed our quiet lives came one awful September evening. A storm was blowing in. The winds were terrible! They howled and whistled around the tall walls of the lighthouse. The waves were **mounting** higher and higher. A little after midnight, my father asked me to help him outside.

"We must secure our belongings, Grace," he said. "The night is going to be nasty."

Steadying myself against the wind, I followed him. We tied up our rowboat. We moved things inside. In a storm like this, anything loose would be blown away.

Then we returned to the safety of the lighthouse. Mum and Dad went to bed, but I couldn't sleep at all. The storm was far too wild and loud.

At around 5:00 A.M., I went up to the top of the lighthouse. Staring out into the sea, I saw something. Out by the Big Harcar Rocks was a huge, dark shape. It looked **eerie** and strange.

Stop Think Write

VOCABULARY

Why might the rocks look <u>eerie</u>?

_____

_____

_____

I ran downstairs and woke father. He came up to look. With the first rays of the sun, the eerie dark shape became clearer. It was a ship, a big one! It looked like a paddleboat steamer. The storm had driven it into the rocks. It was shattered, nearly torn in two!

Had anyone survived?

At first, it was hard to tell. The skies were still gray. The rain continued to come down heavily. Using a telescope, however, we finally saw them. Out on the rock, inches above the waves, people were crawling around.

In this storm, no rescuers could make it from the mainland. The surviving passengers had only one hope: us.

"Father," I said, "We must help them. They won't last long!"

At first, my father said nothing. His look was deadly serious. He was deep in thought. I knew what he was thinking about—the rowboat.

Stop Think Write

UNDERSTANDING CHARACTERS

How can you tell that Grace cares about people?

_____

_____

_____

Our rowboat was about twenty feet long. Normally, it took three or four rowers to handle such a large boat. In calm water, two people could manage it. Now, however, the sea was anything but calm. It was furious. Strong winds had churned up the waves, and they were **frothing**.

My younger brother was on the mainland, and Mother would have to tend to the lighthouse. That left just two of us to row. If we hoped to rescue the passengers, Father and I would have to do it ourselves.

"Let's try, Grace," said my father, breaking his silence. "If we don't, they will surely die."

While climbing into the rowboat, I looked back at the lighthouse. Would I ever see it again? I could see the fear in my mother's eyes as she watched us leave.

We pushed off into the waves as the wind drove rain into our eyes. The waves shoved our tiny boat this way and that, and several times we nearly tipped over. All we could do was pull hard at the oars.

Stop | Think | Write

Why is Grace's mother afraid?

_____

_____

_____

I rowed and rowed. I tried not to think about the boat tipping over, or about the pain in my arms. Somehow we made it to the Big Harcar Rocks. The nine survivors of the shipwreck huddled on the slippery stone. I could see the fear in their eyes. They looked cold and miserable, yet when they saw us, their faces changed. Suddenly they were full of hope.

As they scrambled toward us, my father jumped onto the rock. He held up his hands to stop them. "This boat is small. We can't take you all in one trip," he yelled. He was screaming because the wind was so loud. "Just five now. We'll come back for the rest of you."

As five of the survivors climbed aboard, I tried to **stabilize** the boat to keep it from tipping over. For a second, I thought we might sink. Then my father turned the boat back toward our island. Three of the passengers helped with the oars, so rowing was easier than before.

Stop **Think** **Write**

VOCABULARY

Why is it important for Grace to <u>stabilize</u> the boat?

_____

_____

_____

I slumped back to rest. I don't think I could have pulled one more stroke. Once we reached our island, I helped three of the passengers onto the shore. My father and the three other rowers headed back to pick up those we had left behind.

I led the survivors into the lighthouse. They were shivering and half-drowned after their night on the rock. My mother sat them in front of the fire and covered them with blankets. My father returned with the others a while later, and we began to warm them up, as well.

I was so proud of what we'd done. Still, I never would have expected what happened afterward. News got out about the rescue. At first, just a few visitors came. Then more and more people arrived. They were rowdy reporters, noisy and full of questions. They didn't want to talk to father. They wanted to talk to me!

Stop | Think | Write

UNDERSTANDING CHARACTERS

How does Grace feel about what she and her father did?

_____

_____

_____

The reporters were surprised. How could a young girl row through a wicked storm?

I hadn't realized that this was unusual. Rowing was part of island life for me. However, girls from other places usually didn't row. Every day, I answered questions. I sat and posed while artists painted my picture. Visitors kept coming.

My poor Mum! She spent all of her time keeping the lighthouse clean. She was always worried that a dignified visitor might arrive and find the house in a mess.

My father grumbled that the island was now too busy. "I almost wish I'd never rescued those people," he'd say.

I knew he was joking. He felt the same as I did. If you have the chance to save a life, you must, even if it changes your own.

Stop | Think | Write

CAUSE AND EFFECT

How does life on the island make Grace different from girls in other places?

_____

_____

_____

Look Back and Respond

1 **What kind of person is Grace?**

_____

_____

_____

Hint

Clues are on almost every page!

2 **Why does Grace's father hesitate before deciding to take the rowboat to try to rescue survivors?**

_____

_____

_____

Hint

For clues, see pages 106 and 107.

3 **Why do the reporters pay so much attention to Grace?**

_____

_____

_____

Hint

For a clue, see page 110.

4 **How does the rescue change Grace's life?**

_____

_____

_____

Hint

For clues, see pages 104 and 110.

✓ **TARGET VOCABULARY**

engulf
falter
frail
relishing
undulating

Hot-Air Balloons

1 Even a brave person would **falter** at the thought of circling the globe in a hot-air balloon. Yet, for over a century, people have overcome their hesitations and fears and tried to do just that.

What kind of journey might make you <u>falter</u>?

_____

_____

_____

2 In 1783, the Montgolfier brothers built a balloon out of thin silk, paper, and a basket. Onlookers must have thought they were foolish to put their faith in such a **frail** craft. However, the balloon was able to fly over a mile.

Name an object that looks <u>frail</u> but is surprisingly strong. Explain.

_____

_____

_____

3 The crowd watched the balloon **undulating** in the breeze. It moved slowly up and down with a gentle motion.

What things can make an undulating motion?

_____

_____

_____

4 As a balloon rises higher, clouds may **engulf** it. Higher up, the balloon may break through the clouds and into the sunshine.

What is a synonym for engulf?

_____

_____

5 **Relishing** the freedom of floating in the air, some people make frequent balloon trips. People can even take short balloon trips at fairgrounds.

What is an activity that you have been relishing this year?

_____

_____

_____

High Fliers

by Carol Alexander

High in the snowy mountains of Switzerland, two men watched the skies. Their craft, the *Breitling Orbiter III*, swayed in the wind. The weather had been uncertain. At last, the ground crew gave them the okay.

Bertrand Piccard turned to his co-pilot, Brian Jones. "I think it's time," he said.

News reporters circled the *Breitling Orbiter*. Excitement ran high in the crowd. "If this flight is successful, Piccard and Jones will have made history!" a reporter exclaimed into her microphone. "These two men will attempt to circle the globe in a balloon! People have tried to do this for years, ever since Jules Verne wrote about the idea in his novel *Around the World in Eighty Days.*"

Stop **Think** **Write**

STORY STRUCTURE

What event is the crowd waiting for?

_____

_____

_____

A second reporter added, "That's right. All previous attempts have failed, but maybe this balloon will succeed. Look at it—it's about as tall as the Statue of Liberty! The outer layers of the balloon **engulf** another envelope inside. That one contains helium, which is lighter than air. Surrounding the helium envelope is regular air. The pilots will heat the air to make the balloon ascend."

"Didn't Piccard try before?" a man in the crowd asked.

"Yes, he's actually tried twice before. The third time might be the charm," said the reporter.

The trip would not be easy, but Bertrand Piccard had adventure in his blood. His grandfather had been a hot-air balloonist. Piccard's father had explored the depths of the ocean. They were a family of adventurers.

Stop | Think | Write

AUTHOR'S PURPOSE

Why does the author mention earlier unsuccessful flights?

_____

_____

_____

Piccard was not one to **falter**. He and Jones would put their trust in the winds—and in the ground crew. The ground crew was an important part of their team. They would advise Piccard and Jones of weather conditions and make sure their flight path was cleared with different countries around the world.

The take off was smooth, the balloon **undulating** in the wind. They headed south toward Morocco. The men could not steer, but they could make the balloon go up or down by using propane burners to heat the gas. They had to be careful not to use too much propane, or they wouldn't have enough to finish the trip.

The balloon flew over storm clouds and mountaintops. After reaching Morocco, the balloon went east across the Sahara Desert. Then the men ran into their first problem. The country of Yemen refused to give the balloonists permission to fly over their air space. Piccard and Jones might have to land.

Stop Think Write

What does the author mean when she writes that "Piccard was not one to <u>falter</u>"?

_____

_____

_____

At that moment, the men in the air realized how **frail** their craft really was. The armed forces of Yemen might attempt to shoot them down. However, their luck held out, and they crossed the region safely.

Another balloon that had set out on a round-the-world trip two weeks earlier had not been so lucky. It had been forced to land in the ocean due to ice build-up on its surface. When they heard from the ground crew about the forced landing, Piccard and Jones were concerned. Although the other balloon was no longer their competition, the pilots were their friends. They were glad to find out that the pilots were safely rescued.

There was more trouble for the *Breitling Orbiter* as it neared China. Chinese air traffic control didn't want the balloon to fly over their air space.

Piccard cried, "We spent over a year getting the approval for this part of our trip!"

Stop **Think** **Write**

VOCABULARY

What made Piccard and Jones realize that their balloon was <u>frail</u>?

The next few days were nerve-racking. Would the Chinese stop the balloon? Not everyone on the ground understood how balloons fly. They couldn't be steered like airplanes. Balloon pilots could not predict an exact course. The language problem made things difficult, too.

A week later, the balloon cleared the Chinese border. Next, they would cross the Pacific Ocean. That part of the trip would be longer than the whole way they had come so far. It could be very dangerous because there was no place to land.

Piccard wrote in his diary, "This is exactly my definition of adventure....You have to dig inside yourself to find the courage and resources to deal with what may lie ahead."

The men soon had a decision to make. The clouds to the north could kill them because the temperature might disable the balloon. Going south would add a thousand miles to the trip. Would they have enough fuel?

Stop Think Write

STORY STRUCTURE

Why might the trip across the Pacific Ocean be dangerous?

_____

_____

_____

Heading south, the weather turned harsh. The crew rose high above the clouds to escape it. The air in the cabin grew freezing. The men put on all the clothing they had. They slept in three sleeping bags. It grew very difficult to breathe.

The ground crew told them to use oxygen. The oxygen helped Piccard and Jones, but they encountered another problem. Now, the balloon was running out of fuel. Here they were, on the final leg of the trip. Did they dare try to fly over the Atlantic Ocean? Should they try a landing, or go for it?

Piccard said, "The only way to fail is to quit, and we're not going to quit!"

On the ground, the Swiss news reporters followed the story closely. Would Piccard and Jones make history? Or would they be forced to give up?

Stop | Think | Write

CAUSE AND EFFECT

Why did the crew have to consider whether or not to cross the Atlantic Ocean?

_____

_____

_____

The Atlantic crossing was successful. The balloon was heading over the African continent. Then the radio stopped working. After three weeks of bad food, thin air, and close quarters, the pilots had lost touch with the ground crew.

Miles over the Earth, the men did not even realize they had reached their goal. They had circled the globe. Piccard found a strange beauty in the desert crossing. **Relishing** the view, he told Jones, "Looking over the desert makes up for all of it. To me, the star-filled sky and the sand below are truly magical."

So at last, they landed in the desert of Egypt. They waited in unending miles of sand for the rescue team. An excited reporter asked them, "Did you take anything along for good luck?"

Brian Jones told the reporter, "Yes, we did. We had a book that once belonged to Jules Verne."

Stop | Think | Write

STORY STRUCTURE

Why didn't the crew realize they had completed their trip around the globe?

_____

_____

_____

Look Back and Respond

1 How would you describe Bertrand Piccard?

_____

_____

_____

Hint

For clues, see pages 115, 116, 118, and 119.

2 How does the setting change through the story?

_____

_____

Hint

Clues you can use are on almost every page.

3 What danger did the crew run into as they crossed Yemen?

_____

_____

_____

Hint

For a clue, see pages 116 and 117.

4 Why did Piccard and Jones take a book that had belonged to Jules Verne with them?

_____

_____

_____

Hint

For clues, see pages 114 and 120.

Lesson 13

culmination
expanse
frigid
prime
sacrificed

Polar Exploration

1 In the early 1900s, many explorers traveled to the Arctic. Some tried to reach the North Pole. Reaching the pole would be the **culmination** of an Arctic explorer's dreams. There could be no higher achievement.

Write a synonym for <u>culmination</u>.

_____

2 The Arctic was a vast **expanse** of cold seas and ice. In the late 1800s and early 1900s, explorers tried to map this huge territory. Some also sailed south to explore the region called Antarctica.

Name and describe an <u>expanse</u> of land in your state or community.

_____

_____

_____

3 Early Arctic explorers faced **frigid** weather. Winter temperatures in the Arctic averaged around -30°F (-34°C). In Antarctica, the climate was even colder.

What is the most <u>frigid</u> weather you have ever experienced? How did it affect you?

_____

_____

_____

4 Polar explorers needed to prepare for the harsh climate at the poles. They would **prime** themselves by exercising in high altitudes and hiking in cold, snow-covered regions.

How might runners <u>prime</u> themselves for a big race?

_____

_____

_____

5 Early polar explorers **sacrificed** a great deal. Some went into debt to pay for their trips. They suffered pain and hardship in a cold, dark climate. Most explorers felt that the prize of reaching the North or South Pole was worth great hardship.

Tell about a time when you <u>sacrificed</u> something. Why did you make the sacrifice?

_____

_____

_____

The Race to the South Pole

by Duncan Searl

Roald Amundsen couldn't believe the news. The American explorers Robert Peary and Matthew Henson had just reached the North Pole. This was a disaster for Amundsen.

For two years, he had been carefully planning his own voyage to the North Pole. His ship, the *Fram*, was stocked for the Arctic voyage. His crew was ready. He even had sled dogs.

It had taken great effort to **prime** himself for the trip, but Amundsen saw no reason to go now. He didn't want to be the second person to reach the North Pole. There was no glory in that. There would be no riches either, and that was important. To pay for his voyage, Amundsen had planned to write a book about being the first person to reach the pole.

Standing on the deck of the *Fram*, the thirty-eight-year-old Norwegian explorer slowly turned. He had been staring north. Now, he gazed southward. "Maybe there is another way," he thought.

Stop | Think | Write

MAIN IDEAS AND DETAILS

Why was Robert Peary's success a disaster for Roald Amundsen?

_____

_____

_____

Change of Plans

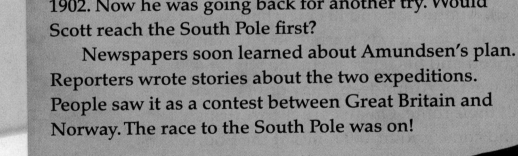

The first person to reach the South Pole would enjoy fame and glory, too. Several explorers had tried, but they had all failed. Roald Amundsen made a sudden decision. Instead of sailing to "the top of the world," he would sail to the bottom!

The *Fram* left Oslo, Norway, in June of 1910. The sailors thought they were sailing north to the Arctic. Once they were out at sea, they learned the truth. Their real destination was Antarctica—12,000 miles to the south!

Amundsen had learned that another explorer was sailing to Antarctica, too. Robert Scott of Great Britain had failed to reach the South Pole in 1902. Now he was going back for another try. Would Scott reach the South Pole first?

Newspapers soon learned about Amundsen's plan. Reporters wrote stories about the two expeditions. People saw it as a contest between Great Britain and Norway. The race to the South Pole was on!

Stop Think Write

MAIN IDEAS AND DETAILS

Why was Robert Scott a problem for Roald Amundsen?

_____

_____

_____

Winter in the Antarctic

On January 11, 1911, the *Fram* reached the Ross Ice Shelf in Antarctica. This **expanse** of ice lies 760 miles from the South Pole. The Norwegians built a hut on the ice. They unloaded their supplies and dogs. Only seven men stayed with Amundsen. The others sailed to Argentina before ice could trap the ship.

The long winter began. There would be six months of total darkness. Inside their hut, the explorers wondered what lay ahead. They would be traveling through unmapped territory to reach the South Pole. They didn't know what obstacles they might find.

In August, the sunlight finally returned. In September, however, the temperature was still a **frigid** -63° F (-53°C). Amundsen and his men had to wait another month before it was warm enough to travel.

Robert Scott and his team spent the winter 400 miles to the west of Amundsen. They didn't have to worry about their route. On an earlier trip, British explorers had come within 100 miles of the South Pole. Captain Scott planned to go the same way this time.

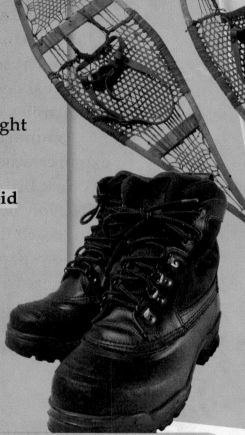

Stop	Think	Write

VOCABULARY

Why was frigid weather a problem for the explorers?

_____

_____

_____

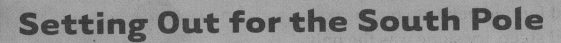

Setting Out for the South Pole

On October 20, Roald Amundsen and four companions loaded their dogsleds. Strapping on their skis, they set out. Despite snowy weather, the Norwegians made good progress on the ice shelf. Sometimes, the sled dogs even towed the men and the sleds.

In the distance, however, a problem loomed. The Queen Maud Mountains came into view. These high peaks blocked Amundsen's path, for the South Pole sat on a high plateau on the other side of the mountains.

Captain Scott's party didn't start out until November 3. Their expedition was large, with sixteen men, thirteen sleds, twenty-three dogs, and ten ponies. Scott's group moved slowly. Two of the sleds had motors, but they broke down. The ponies had trouble walking on ice, and they slowed the progress of the dogsleds. To make matters worse, a snowstorm stopped Scott for five days.

Stop Think Write

COMPARE AND CONTRAST

How was Robert Scott's expedition different from Roald Amundsen's?

_____

_____

_____

Rough Going

Near the mountains, Roald Amundsen spotted a long streak of ice. A glacier, 10,000 feet high, had formed between two peaks. Climbing that steep, icy slope was the only way to cross the mountains.

The struggle up the glacier took days. Two teams of dogs were needed to pull each sled. The men had to push the sleds, too. Deep, wide cracks in the ice made the climb dangerous.

At the top of the glacier, the Norwegians buried supplies for their return journey. Then they **sacrificed** their weakest dogs to provide food. This was sad but necessary for their survival.

To the west, Robert Scott also faced a glacier. Before climbing it, he sacrificed his ponies for food. Then he sent all the dogs and empty sleds back to his base camp.

Scott's glacier wasn't as steep as Amundsen's. However, the climb was exhausting. Without dogs, the men had to drag their heavy sleds. One man fell down a deep hole in the ice. By the time Scott reached the top of the glacier, it was December 25, 1911.

Stop **Think** **Write**

Why were dogs and ponies <u>sacrificed</u> by the explorers?

_____

_____

_____

Success!

Once they passed the glacier, Amundsen and his men skied south. Just 250 miles of level land separated them from their goal. Each day, they looked for signs of the British. Was Captain Scott ahead of them?

On December 13, 1911, the explorers were just fifteen miles from the South Pole. The **culmination** of years of planning was near. Amundsen was too excited to sleep. To prepare for reaching the South Pole, he tied a Norwegian flag to his ski pole.

The next day, Amundsen planted that flag at 90° south—the South Pole. For two days, the explorers circled for miles around the spot. They took measurements and observed the sun. They made absolutely sure they were at the right place.

Captain Scott, of course, was behind Amundsen. The British explorers didn't reach the South Pole until January 17, 1912. There they saw the Norwegian flag. "It is a terrible disappointment," Scott wrote.

Stop | **Think** | **Write**

MAIN IDEAS AND DETAILS

How did Roald Amundsen make sure he was really at the South Pole?

_____

_____

_____

Homeward Bound

Amundsen's return trip went without a hitch. The weather remained sunny. The dogs helped pull the skiers. Once down the glacier, everyone raced across the ice shelf. The *Fram* was waiting, and on January 25, 1912, the explorers were on board.

Amundsen sailed to South America. There, he published reports about his trip. He later traveled the world giving speeches. He also wrote a best-selling book. Amundsen earned enough money to pay for his expedition and to pay for more adventures, too.

Tragically, Robert Scott never did return from the Antarctic. During his homeward trek, a blizzard struck. By then, the British explorers were exhausted from pulling their sleds. They tried to wait out the storm in a tent, but their food and fuel ran out.

Roald Amundsen and Robert Scott bravely challenged an icy climate and unknown terrain in order to reach the South Pole. Their achievements encouraged others to explore Antarctica. Each year, scientists learn more and more about this important continent.

Stop | Think | Write

MAIN IDEAS AND DETAILS

Why didn't Robert Scott and his party return from their journey to the South Pole?

_____

_____

_____

Look Back and Respond

1 In just a few sentences, describe what this text is about.

_____

_____

_____

Hint

Include only the most important information in your response.

2 In 1910, Roald Amundsen suddenly decided to go to the South Pole, not the North Pole. What factors influenced him and made the trip possible?

_____

_____

_____

Hint

For clues, see pages 124 and 125.

3 Why do you think that Roald Amundsen, not Robert Scott, won the race to the South Pole?

_____

_____

_____

Hint

For clues, see pages 127, 128, and 129.

4 What might someone like Roald Amundsen do in today's world? Explain.

_____

_____

_____

Hint

Think about what kind of person Amundsen was.

✓ **TARGET VOCABULARY**

aim
emulate
motive
skeptical
understatement

More Than a Teacher

Many teachers do more than teach. Their enthusiasm and curiosity make them great role models for their students. Students often **1** _____ their teachers by working hard and showing interest in their studies. A teacher's primary **2** _____ is for students to become lifelong learners.

Some students are ③ _____
of their abilities to do well in school. Teachers
might offer a prize to encourage these students
to work extra hard on a project or a test. The
prize gives students a ④ _____
to work extra hard to do a good job.

One teacher gave a pizza party for the students
who showed the greatest improvement. It
would be an ⑤ _____ to
say that the winners were pleased. They were
absolutely thrilled!

Raúl's Landscape

by Mia Lewis

Bold charcoal lines streaked up the page to a copper-colored sky. Raúl gazed out his bedroom window at the urban landscape. His fingers flew across the page as he added details and highlights to his drawing. Sometimes Raúl tried to **emulate** the colors and shapes that his art teacher, Mrs. Hernandez, liked to use. Today, however, the style of his sketch was entirely his own.

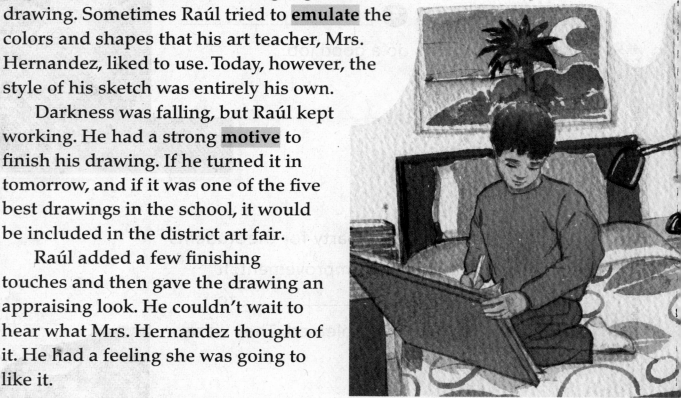

Darkness was falling, but Raúl kept working. He had a strong **motive** to finish his drawing. If he turned it in tomorrow, and if it was one of the five best drawings in the school, it would be included in the district art fair.

Raúl added a few finishing touches and then gave the drawing an appraising look. He couldn't wait to hear what Mrs. Hernandez thought of it. He had a feeling she was going to like it.

Stop **Think** **Write**

VOCABULARY

In what ways might Raúl emulate his art teacher?

_____

_____

_____

134

"Raúl, are you done with your homework?" his mother called. "It's time for the twins to go to bed."

Raúl's mom came into the room with a pajama-clad boy on each hip. Raúl called the twins "double trouble," because they were always into something. At the moment, they were too sleepy to cause trouble. Raúl and his mother tucked José and Luis into their cribs. Then Raúl finished his homework and went to bed.

The next morning, Raúl thought about how to get his drawing safely to school without folding or wrinkling it.

"What about the cardboard tube from the wrapping paper?" suggested his mom. "It's in my room."

Raúl checked that the twins were occupied before dashing into his mother's room to retrieve the roll. When he returned, Raúl's eyes bulged. The twins had his drawing and were scribbling all over it.

Stop | Think | Write

AUTHOR'S PURPOSE

What purpose might the author have for including Raúl's nickname for the twins?

_____

_____

_____

"Oh, no!" Raúl yelled. He snatched his drawing and the charcoal pencils from the twins. "Mom! They've ruined my drawing! What a disaster!"

"Calm down," his mom said gently. "Did you make it for a special assignment? I'm sure your teacher will understand if you explain what happened."

"Special assignment?" said Raúl. "That's an **understatement**! That drawing was my only chance to be chosen for the district art fair. If the drawing isn't submitted to the district art fair, then I'll miss out on the state art fair, too!"

His mom said that she was sure everything would be all right once he explained what had happened to Mrs. Hernandez. Raúl wasn't so sure. He was subdued on the way to school. His friends had made drawings, but to them, the art fair was simply a lark. For Raúl, the art fair was like the World Series. He was at the top of the league—and ready for the championship game!

Stop **Think** **Write**

AUTHOR'S PURPOSE

What does the author mean when she says Raúl was at the top of the league and ready for the championship game?

_____

_____

_____

As soon as he got to school, Raúl went to find Mrs. Hernandez. He unrolled the ruined drawing and told her what had happened. Mrs. Hernandez seemed as crestfallen as Raúl.

"Raúl," she said, "haven't I always taught you to work through problems? You've learned not to give up on a drawing until you get it right, and I don't want you to give up on this, either. You're a talented artist, and my **aim** is to find a way for you to enter the district art fair."

"I believe there's a way you can still enter the contest," Mrs. Hernandez continued. "Mr. Wang, the principal, and I will choose the five best drawings from each grade after school. We will be bringing those winners to the Art Institute of Chicago, where they will be displayed with the entries from other schools. If you can bring us another landscape by the time we start reviewing our entries, we will be able to consider your drawing, too."

Stop Think Write

VOCABULARY

Do you think Raúl shares the same <u>aim</u> as Mrs. Hernandez? Explain.

_____

_____

_____

Mrs. Hernandez had always encouraged Raúl, and he had learned a lot since she had become his teacher. It made him feel good to know that she believed in him, but he was still **skeptical**. How could he possibly finish another drawing during the school day?

Raúl slaved over his drawing every spare minute that day. Mrs. Hernandez set up a table for him, and he worked there while he nibbled on his lunch and during study hall. Mrs. Hernandez even arranged for him to skip gym class so that he could spend more time on his drawing. (He promised to make up the class the next day.) His landscape was taking shape again, but slowly!

Too soon, the last bell of the day rang. Raúl ran to the art room and kept drawing. Then Mr. Wang showed up, and it was time for the judging. Raúl's landscape was so close to being done that it hurt to think about it! Raúl turned away from the teachers and wiped his eyes.

Stop | Think | Write

How does the author show us that Mrs. Hernandez is an important person to Raúl?

_____

_____

_____

Mr. Wang and Mrs. Hernandez looked at all the drawings. They spoke quietly together before returning to the table where Raúl stood.

"Even though your landscape is not quite done, it's still one of the best drawings here," said Mr. Wang. "Do you think you can complete it and bring it to the Art Institute by nine o'clock tonight?"

Raúl was ecstatic. "I'm not about to give up now!" he said. "I'll do my best to get it there on time." He thanked the teachers, rolled up his picture, and headed home as fast as he could. He ran to his room and worked without stopping until the drawing was finished.

Now, he and his dad just had to make it to the Art Institute before nine o'clock. It was already after eight. Raúl's mom was at class. That meant two cranky and sleepy little boys had to come with them across town.

Stop **Think** **Write**

INFER AND PREDICT

How do you think Raúl feels when he and his dad start out for the Art Institute?

_____

_____

_____

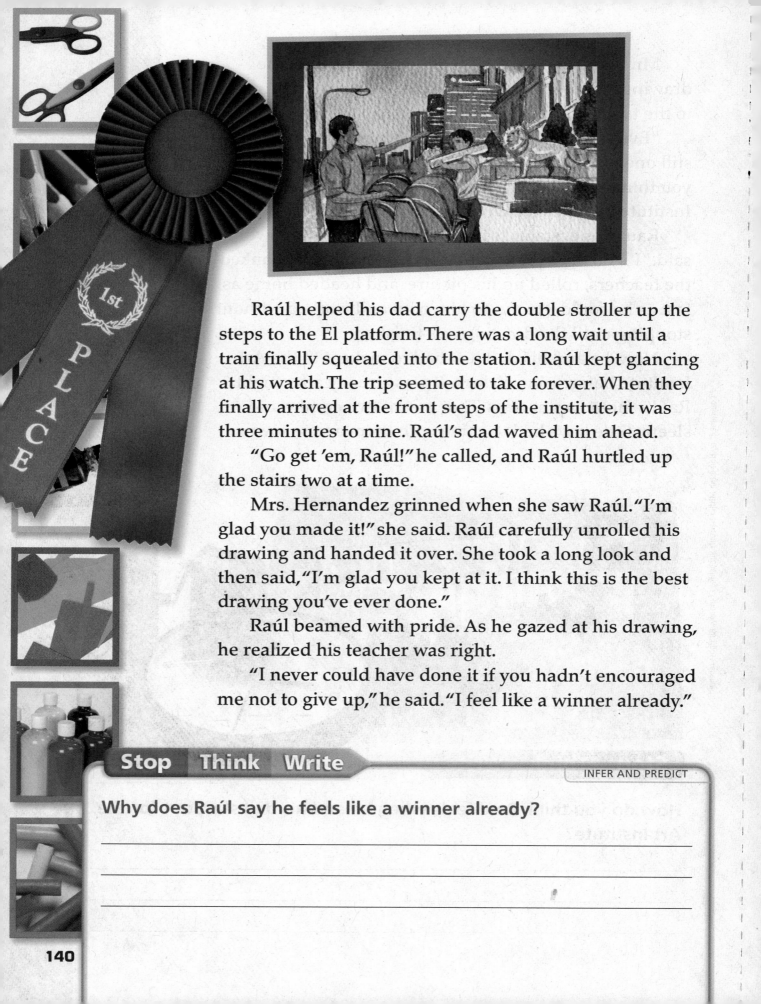

Raúl helped his dad carry the double stroller up the steps to the El platform. There was a long wait until a train finally squealed into the station. Raúl kept glancing at his watch. The trip seemed to take forever. When they finally arrived at the front steps of the institute, it was three minutes to nine. Raúl's dad waved him ahead.

"Go get 'em, Raúl!" he called, and Raúl hurtled up the stairs two at a time.

Mrs. Hernandez grinned when she saw Raúl. "I'm glad you made it!" she said. Raúl carefully unrolled his drawing and handed it over. She took a long look and then said, "I'm glad you kept at it. I think this is the best drawing you've ever done."

Raúl beamed with pride. As he gazed at his drawing, he realized his teacher was right.

"I never could have done it if you hadn't encouraged me not to give up," he said. "I feel like a winner already."

Stop | Think | Write

INFER AND PREDICT

Why does Raúl say he feels like a winner already?

_____

_____

_____

Look Back and Respond

1 What is the main message the author expresses in this story? Explain.

_____

_____

_____

Hint

For clues, see pages 137 and 140. What advice does Mrs. Hernandez give Raúl?

2 How does the author show that Raúl is serious about his art?

_____

_____

_____

Hint

Clues are on almost every page.

3 Reread the last paragraph on page 138. Why does Raúl turn away and wipe his eyes?

_____

_____

_____

Hint

Think about how you would feel if you were Raúl.

4 Why do Mr. Wang and Mrs. Hernandez decide to include Raúl's drawing with the winners?

_____

_____

_____

Hint

For a clue, see page 139.

✓ TARGET VOCABULARY

ascent
hovering
lunar
option
perilous

Driving on the Moon

A lunar rover

1 Some Apollo missions carried **lunar** rovers. These vehicles helped astronauts explore bigger areas of the Moon's surface.

If you could make a <u>lunar</u> vehicle, what would you include in your design?

_____

_____

_____

2 A rover could carry two astronauts and travel uphill, downhill, and on flat surfaces. Traveling uphill required the most power, so the rover's four electric motors worked especially hard during an **ascent**.

Think about a time you walked over a hill or up a mountain. What was the <u>ascent</u> like?

_____

_____

_____

3 Driving a lunar rover on the Moon was **perilous**. If the rover broke down, the astronauts had to hope they could repair it themselves. They relied on their space suits to protect them from the Moon's atmosphere, which is cold and has no oxygen.

What do you think is the most perilous part of a space trip?

_____

_____

_____

4 Modern lunar rovers can travel more than fifty miles. Astronauts have the **option** to travel far from where they land, but they might choose to stay close to their spacecraft. If the lunar rover breaks down, they would not have to walk far to get back.

Tell about a time when you had to decide between a few possible choices. Which option did you choose?

_____

_____

_____

5 Astronauts on the Moon could see Earth. At times, our planet looked as if it were **hovering** over the lunar horizon.

What is the difference between hovering over the ground and flying back and forth in the air?

_____

_____

_____

The Lunar Module
Engineered to Serve
by John Berry

Project Apollo was a series of space flights carried out in the 1960s and 1970s. The main goal was to land a person on the Moon. Success came on July 20, 1969, when astronauts Neil Armstrong and Buzz Aldrin landed a **lunar** *module named* Eagle *on the Moon.*

Q: What is a lunar module?

A: A lunar module (LM) is a small, light craft that can take off from and land on the Moon. *Eagle* was one of fourteen LMs made for the Apollo project. The success of the project depended on these amazing machines. Some people think that LMs are the greatest engineering achievement of the last hundred years.

Q: How big is a lunar module?

A: Early LMs were about twenty-three feet tall. They measured about thirty feet across and weighed about 32,000 pounds. Later LMs were bigger.

Stop | Think | Write

TEXT AND GRAPHIC FEATURES

How do the photographs on this page help you understand more about the purpose of Project Apollo?

_____

_____

_____

Q: Why did people build lunar modules?

A: Scientists were curious about the Moon. They had many questions about how it was formed. In order to answer the questions, people needed to travel to the Moon. Spacecraft were taking people into space, but they could not land on the Moon. Lunar modules were designed and built to do that job.

Q: Why didn't earlier spaceships land on the Moon?

A: They were too heavy. In the early Apollo trips, astronauts traveled in spacecraft called command modules (CMs). The CMs had to carry astronauts safely back to Earth, but the return trip was **perilous**. The CMs got very hot as they entered Earth's atmosphere, so they had to have heat shields. The shields made the CMs too heavy to land on the Moon. If men hoped to walk on the Moon, they would need a lighter craft.

A command module

Stop **Think** **Write**

VOCABULARY

What made the return trip to Earth perilous?

_____

_____

_____

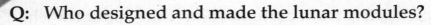
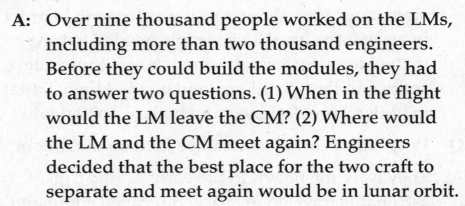

Q: Who designed and made the lunar modules?

A: Over nine thousand people worked on the LMs, including more than two thousand engineers. Before they could build the modules, they had to answer two questions. (1) When in the flight would the LM leave the CM? (2) Where would the LM and the CM meet again? Engineers decided that the best place for the two craft to separate and meet again would be in lunar orbit.

Q: How long did it take to come up with a design?

A: People worked for over five years before the first LM went into space. They started in 1963. Workers researched what the LM would need. Then they designed the parts, built them, and put them together.

Engineers had to make a lot of decisions. Which piece or tool would be lighter? Which would be safer? Which parts were necessary? They had to consider each **option** before making a decision. They performed tests and made changes until they were satisfied.

The first complete LM went into space in 1968. That was a test run. There was no Moon landing. Fourteen lunar modules were built, but only some of them landed on the Moon.

A lunar module on the Moon

Stop | **Think** | **Write**

VOCABULARY

What did engineers think about as they considered each **option** for the LM?

_____

_____

_____

Q: What happened during a typical Apollo flight?

A: Imagine that you are right there, watching it all. The rocket blasts three astronauts into space. Parts of the rocket fall away until just the command module and the lunar module remain.

After passing behind the Moon, the spacecraft moves into orbit around the Moon. Two astronauts enter the LM, leaving the third astronaut behind in the CM. The lunar module separates from the command module. As it falls toward the Moon, rockets fire. They slow the fall of the LM. The LM seems to be **hovering** above the surface. At last it lands on the Moon.

The astronauts do tests, gather rocks and dirt, and explore. They also unload anything from the LM that is no longer needed. The craft needs to be as light as possible for the next part of the trip.

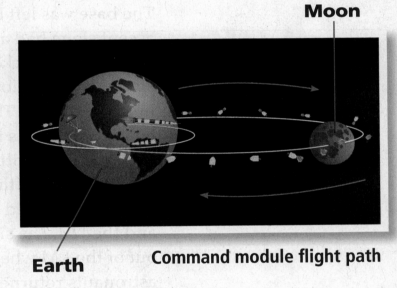

Moon

Earth

Command module flight path

Stop **Think** **Write**

SEQUENCE OF EVENTS

What happens between the time the spacecraft moves into lunar orbit and the moment the LM lands on the Moon?

_____

_____

_____

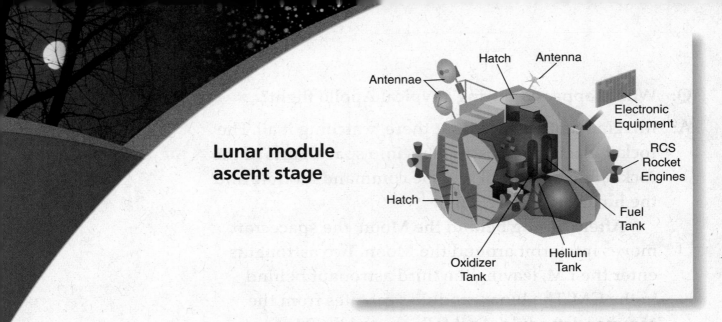

Lunar module
ascent stage

Antennae

Hatch

Antenna

Electronic
Equipment

RCS
Rocket
Engines

Hatch

Fuel
Tank

Oxidizer
Tank

Helium
Tank

Q: How did astronauts return to the CM?

A: The top of the lunar module was called the **ascent** stage. It took astronauts back to the CM. The base was left behind. The outside of the ascent stage had a Rocket Control System (RCS): sixteen small rocket engines that were used for steering. They allowed the pilot to move the LM in any direction. The LM also had antennae. They let the astronauts talk with each other, with the CM, and even with people back on Earth.

Key parts of the LM were its two hatches. The top hatch allowed men to move between the CM and the LM. The side hatch was for getting in and out of the LM when it was on the Moon. Once astronauts returned to the CM, the ascent stage fell back to the Moon.

Stop Think Write

MAIN IDEAS AND DETAILS

What were some key parts of the ascent stage? What was the purpose of each part?

_____

_____

_____

Q: Was the cabin of the LM cramped? Where did the astronauts sit?

A: They didn't. There was no room for seats. The floor space was less than five feet (1.5 m) by five feet (1.5 m), so the astronauts stood up during flights. The LM had oxygen, air pressure, and a comfortable temperature, so the astronauts didn't have to wear their bulky space suits.

Q: Were there any major problems with the LMs?

A: No. The LMs worked very well. They served the Apollo project and took care of the astronauts. This shows the care with which they were designed, built, and tested. It may seem like a shame that most of the LMs had to be left in space.

Q: Where are the Apollo lunar modules today?

A: The table on the next page shows what happened to all fourteen LMs. You can visit the ones that are in museums.

Ascent stage

Lunar module stages

Stop **Think** **Write**

TEXT AND GRAPHIC FEATURES

How does the illustration help you understand more about the LM?

_____

_____

_____

Where Are They Now?

LM	Mission	Current Location
1	Apollo 5	Unknown
2	not used	The National Air and Space Museum, Washington, D.C.
3 Spider	Apollo 9	Jettisoned in space
4 Snoopy	Apollo 10	In orbit around the Sun
5 Eagle	Apollo 11	Moon
6 Intrepid	Apollo 12	Moon
7 Aquarius	Apollo 13	Burned up in Earth's atmosphere
8 Antares	Apollo 14	Moon
9	not used	Kennedy Space Center, Orsino, Florida
10 Falcon	Apollo 15	Moon
11 Orion	Apollo 16	Moon
12 Challenger	Apollo 17	Moon
13	not used	The Cradle of Aviation Museum, Garden City, New York
14	not used	The Franklin Institute, Philadelphia, Pennsylvania

Stop   Think   Write

TEXT AND GRAPHIC FEATURES

Where did many of the lunar modules end up?

_____

_____

_____

Look Back and Respond

1 How does the title help you understand the article?

_____

_____

_____

Hint

For clues, see pages 144, 145, and 146.

2 What might scientists hope to learn by sending astronauts to the Moon to do tests, collect samples, and explore?

_____

_____

_____

Hint

For clues, see page 145.

3 Why was the LM's ascent stage so important to the mission?

_____

_____

_____

Hint

For clues, see page 148.

4 How do you think the author feels about lunar modules? Explain.

_____

_____

_____

Hint

For clues, see pages 144 and 149.

The Vikings

**ancestral
destiny
ruthless
saga
unearthed**

1 The homeland of the Vikings was Scandinavia. Today, Scandinavia includes the countries of Norway, Sweden, and Finland. In the ninth century, many Vikings left their **ancestral** lands to settle in Iceland.

Why might people leave their <u>ancestral</u> homes?

_____

_____

_____

2 Vikings carried out raids in foreign lands. They could be **ruthless**, showing no pity for the people they raided. However, some Vikings were farmers who cared for their families and were merciful to others.

What word in the paragraph is an antonym for <u>ruthless</u>?

_____

3 Erik the Red was a bold Viking who explored and settled in Greenland. The long **saga** of his life, brave deeds, and adventures has been retold many times.

How is a <u>saga</u> different from other stories?

_____

_____

_____

4 The Vikings tried several times to settle in North America. They may have thought it was their **destiny** to live there. However, they did not establish a permanent colony. The Vikings eventually left North America.

When we say something is our <u>destiny</u>, what do we mean?

_____

_____

_____

5 Scientists have **unearthed** the remains of a Viking settlement in North America. Nails, lamps, and other artifacts at the site give clues to how the Vikings lived.

What kinds of things might be <u>unearthed</u> at the site of an ancient settlement?

_____

_____

_____

Erik the Red
and Viking Exploration

by Claire Daniel

Five hundred years before Christopher Columbus "discovered" North America, the Vikings landed there. North America was thousands of miles from the Viking homeland of Scandinavia. However, Viking explorers had a long tradition of traveling beyond their **ancestral** land. In the eighth and ninth centuries, they led raids to England, Ireland, Wales, and Spain. Viking explorers then sailed from Europe to explore the territory across the Atlantic Ocean.

One of the best-known Viking explorers was Erik the Red. His real name was Eirikr Thorvaldson, but he earned the nickname Erik the Red because of his red hair and beard. His **saga** has been told for hundreds of years.

Erik was born in Norway around the year 935. When he was still young, his father left Norway with his family. They sailed to Iceland, which had recently been settled by the Vikings. Erik's family built a farm there.

Stop | **Think** | **Write**

VOCABULARY

What does it mean to call a place your <u>ancestral</u> land?

_____

_____

_____

Westward to Greenland

Erik married a woman from a well-to-do family. As a wedding gift, her father gave the couple a good piece of farmland. Erik's wife said that he was a good husband who farmed well and was kind to her. However, Erik had conflicts with some neighbors that led to violence. In about the year 981, he was banished from Iceland as punishment for his **ruthless** behavior.

Erik the Red set off on a ship, sailing west. He discovered a land that he called Greenland. For a few years, he traveled to different parts of the land. In his opinion, Greenland had even better farmland than Iceland. Erik decided that he wanted to create a permanent settlement in the new land.

Greenland   Iceland

Stop | Think | Write

COMPARE AND CONTRAST

How did Erik's behavior toward his wife differ from his behavior toward his neighbors?

_____

_____

_____

A New Settlement

Erik the Red returned to Iceland, hoping to convince others to join him in Greenland. His stories about the new land excited people. Before long, other Viking families wanted to settle in Greenland.

In 985, Erik led a group of Vikings to Greenland. Men, women, and children boarded twenty-five ships. They brought cattle, sheep, horses, pigs, and dogs with them. They loaded up dried fish and meat, cheese, and butter. They packed farming tools, tents, hunting gear, and kitchen tools.

No one knows how many people left with Erik the Red. Historians think as many as 600 Vikings may have gone. However, the voyage was difficult. Of the twenty-five ships that set off, only fourteen arrived in Greenland. The others either turned back or sank.

| Stop | Think | Write |

CONCLUSIONS AND GENERALIZATIONS

Why did the Vikings bring so many animals and supplies with them to Greenland?

_____

_____

_____

An Accidental Discovery

In 986, a trader named Bjarni Herjólfsson left Iceland to join his family in Greenland. He had no compass. His sailors depended on the stars to find their way. Cloudy days and nights made navigation difficult. The sailors veered off course and sailed southwest of Greenland.

There, the trader sighted a new land. Although he did not set foot on the land, he told others about it when he reached Greenland. Many people today believe this new land was what we now call Newfoundland, on the eastern coast of Canada. If so, Herjólfsson had seen North America.

Two people were very interested in the trader's stories: Erik the Red and his son, Leif. Leif offered to buy the trader's ship, and Herjólfsson eventually agreed. Leif wanted to use the ship to sail to the new land that Herjólfsson had seen.

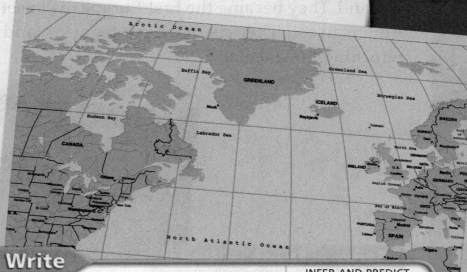

Stop | Think | Write

INFER AND PREDICT

Explain how Herjólfsson's discovery of the new land was accidental.

_____

_____

_____

Exploring Vinland

Erik the Red intended to travel with his son on this new adventure. However, shortly before the trip was to begin, Erik injured his leg. Viking sailors were very superstitious. Erik thought the broken leg was a bad sign. He may have decided it was not his **destiny** to explore the new land. In the end, he chose not to go on the trip.

Leif reached the new land and sailed south along the coast. First, he saw a land that had flat stones, which was probably the Baffin Islands. He kept sailing. Next, he saw a wooded land with a white beach. He called it "Markland." It was probably the south shore of Labrador.

Leif sailed on until he reached a third place. This land had fields, woods, pastures, and grapevines. He called it "Vinland." Leif and his crew stepped ashore at Vinland. They became the first Europeans to set foot on American soil. They spent the winter at Vinland before returning to Greenland.

Stop | Think | Write

VOCABULARY

Why might Erik the Red have thought it was not his destiny to explore the new land?

_____

_____

_____

A Family of Explorers

Erik the Red had four children: Leif, Thorvald, Thorstein, and Freydis. They all left Greenland to explore North America. After Leif's return, Thorvald sailed to Vinland and explored the nearby coasts. He fought with local American Indians. During one fight, an arrow struck and killed him.

Leif's brother Thorstein led another group of Vikings to America, but they did not stay. Yet another group of Vikings tried to establish a colony in Vinland, but fighting with American Indians proved too dangerous. The group packed up and left.

Erik the Red's daughter, Freydis, was part of a later group that tried to settle in Vinland. Fighting led to the failure of this settlement, too. However, the fighting wasn't against American Indians. People from Iceland fought against people from Greenland!

Despite many tries, the Vikings couldn't create a permanent colony in Vinland. Even so, the adventures of Erik the Red and his family have been told over and over since that time.

Stop | Think | Write

COMPARE AND CONTRAST

How were the troubles of Freydis's group different from problems encountered by previous Viking groups in Vinland?

_____

_____

_____

Where Was Vinland?

No one knows the exact location of Vinland. Some people think it was where Cape Cod, Massachusetts, is now. Others believe it was in Newfoundland, Canada.

* * * * *

In 1960, scientists **unearthed** remains of a Viking colony in Newfoundland. The scientists found eight buildings at the site. They also found boat sheds and large outdoor pits for cooking meat. Among the artifacts at the site were nails, a lamp, an anvil stone, and a spindle. The spindle proved that women lived there and used the spindle to spin wool into yarn.

Today you can visit the remains of the Viking settlement. It is called L'Anse aux Meadows. Many people think the settlement must be Vinland, but there is no way to know for sure.

Stop Think Write

MAIN IDEAS AND DETAILS

Which artifact helps us understand the role that women played in the Viking settlement we now call L'Anse aux Meadows? Explain.

_____

_____

_____

Look Back and Respond

1 Why might Erik the Red have been glad that he was banished from Iceland?

_____

_____

_____

Hint

For clues, see pages 155 and 156.

2 How was the Viking settlement of Greenland different from the Viking settlement of Vinland?

_____

_____

_____

Hint

For clues, see pages 156, 158, and 159.

3 What important accomplishment did Erik's son Leif achieve?

_____

_____

_____

_____

Hint

For clues, see page 158.

4 In what way were Erik the Red's children alike?

_____

_____

_____

Hint

For clues, see page 159.

archaeologists
distinct
elaborate
lustrous
replicas

Clues to the Past

Some scientists work to discover how people lived in the past. **Archaeologists** search for things that may have been buried for years. They look for the ruins of buildings or for other **distinct** objects, such as bowls and tools.

To accomplish this, the scientists often set up **elaborate** digs. They carefully plan and carry out every detail. They mark off areas where they will work. Then they slowly dig down through the ground. They often find very valuable items, such as necklaces and rings made of **lustrous** gold. Sometimes they find the ruins of buildings.

The things the scientists find often end up in museums. Sometimes, though, items are too valuable to display. A museum may display **replicas** of the items instead.

1. Scientists called _____ work to find things that have been buried for years.

2. Sometimes archaeologists find very valuable items, such as jewelry made of _____ gold.

3. Other _____ objects, such as cups and tools, tell us how people lived in the past.

4. Many digs are very _____ and must be carefully planned and carried out.

5. Describe some replicas you own or have seen.

   _____

   _____

   _____

6. Your teacher tells you that your school's new library has an elaborate floor plan. What does this mean?

   _____

   _____

   _____

The Great Wall of China

by Richard Stull

One of the world's most amazing man-made structures is known as the Great Wall of China. This huge wall stretches over the countryside in northern China. People call the wall "great" for a good reason. It is about 4,500 miles (7,300 km) long!

The Great Wall starts near the Pacific coast. From there, it runs and twists westward. It crosses deserts, hills, and mountains. Along the way, it varies in size. The wall is generally about twenty-five feet high. Its base is from fifteen to thirty feet wide. The top of the wall is from nine to twelve feet wide.

When was the Great Wall built? Why was it built? Who built it? How was it made? Thanks to the work of **archaeologists** who have studied the Great Wall, we know a lot about the history of this remarkable structure.

Stop | Think | Write

FACT AND OPINION

Does the first sentence of the article state a fact or an opinion? Explain.

_____

_____

_____

Early History of the Great Wall

People may be surprised to learn that the Great Wall is not just one wall. It is an **elaborate** system of many walls. The first walls were built in the seventh century B.C.E. Some of the walls were several miles long. More long walls were built over the next three hundred years in different parts of what is now northern China.

By the third century B.C.E., many walls had been built throughout the northern kingdoms. Some of the walls ran east to west. Others ran north to south.

By 221 B.C.E., the northern kingdom of Qin had conquered many neighboring kingdoms. The ruler of Qin was named Qin Shihuang. This ruler ordered many smaller walls in his new empire to be torn down. He then ordered workers to link other **distinct** walls in the north. The result was a long wall that ran along the northern border of Qin. It separated China from the rest of northern Asia.

Stop Think Write

VOCABULARY

What does the word <u>elaborate</u> tell about the system of walls?

_____

_____

_____

During the rule of Qin Shihuang, thousands of soldiers guarded the Great Wall. After his death, though, the wall was neglected. It soon fell into ruin.

Why the Walls Were Built

Kings had the first walls built to protect their castles and kingdoms. The people feared attacks from neighboring kingdoms. They were also scared of attacks from other countries in Asia.

For hundreds of years after Qin Shihuang's death, new walls were built in other parts of the country. These walls were built to protect the people from attack. However, the walls soon began to serve a second purpose.

Trade with other countries had become a big business in China. Traders carried **lustrous** silks and spices from China to other countries. The traders traveled by horse, camel, and cart.

Stop **Think** **Write**

CAUSE AND EFFECT

Why were the early parts of the Great Wall built?

_____

_____

_____

Some of the walls stood along the roads used by the traders. Soldiers who guarded the walls could protect the traders as they passed. Because such care was taken to protect the traders, some people think Chinese rulers cared more about the traders than they did about their own people.

The Great Wall did not always prove to be a good defense against attack. Warring armies simply marched through the land where no walls stood.

How the Early Walls Were Built

Today, it seems difficult to believe that workers built the Great Wall entirely by hand. They did, though. Large wooden frames were used to build the early walls. Workers first set the frames in place. Then they began filling the frames with dirt, stones, and other materials. As they slowly filled the frame, workers packed the mixture by stamping on it with their feet. This made the walls strong.

Stop | **Think** | **Write**

FACT AND OPINION

Which sentence in the first paragraph states an opinion? Explain.

_____

_____

_____

The materials used for each section of the wall depended on the location of the wall. Walls in desert regions were made mostly of packed earth. Walls that ran through grasslands were made of dirt, plants, and stones. Walls in mountain regions were made by stacking large stones on top of one another.

The kings and emperors ordered people from around the kingdom to work on the wall. The people had no choice. They were probably no better off than slaves. Over the years, as many as two or three million Chinese laborers may have worked on the wall.

The Great Wall We Know Today

By 1450, rulers started building a series of new walls. The new walls ran along the northern border of China. These walls were larger than the earlier ones. They were also stronger because they were made of bricks.

Stop | Think | Write

MAIN IDEAS AND DETAILS

What effect did using bricks have on walls that were built after 1450?

_____

_____

_____

The workers also repaired some of the old walls along the border. These old walls had been in ruins for hundreds of years. Huge gates connected parts of the new and old walls. Watchtowers and forts were built along the walls. Thousands of soldiers lived in the forts. The new, stronger Great Wall was more effective against enemy attacks.

In time, China and its neighbors to the north became friendlier with one another. Fewer wars made the Great Wall less important than it had been in the past. As a result, the walls were not repaired as often as they had been. The new version of the Great Wall met the same fate as the earlier versions. It fell into ruin.

Stop | Think | Write

Why did the new version of the Great Wall finally fall into ruin?

_____

_____

_____

Visiting the Great Wall

In the last century, the Chinese started to repair parts of the Great Wall. They worked mainly on parts near Beijing, China's capital. They have also repaired sections of the wall that are many miles from the capital.

Thousands of tourists visit the restored sections of the Great Wall each year. They can walk along the wall. They can look inside the towers. From the top of the wall, they can enjoy the beauty of the surrounding landscape. They can visit shops where they can buy plastic or paper **replicas** of the Great Wall.

As they walk along, visitors should think about the long history of what they are standing on. They should think about the country that has changed over the years. They should reflect on the rulers who have come and gone. Last, but not least, they should pause to think of the millions of people who worked so hard to create the Great Wall of China.

Stop | Think | Write

VOCABULARY

Why might visitors to the Great Wall want to buy replicas of the wall?

_____

_____

_____

Look Back and Respond

1 Archaeologists study items left behind by people from the past. What might archaeologists have discovered that helps us know about the Great Wall?

Hint

For clues, see pages 165, 166, 167, and 168.

_____

_____

_____

2 What were the main uses of the Great Wall in the past?

Hint

For clues, see pages 166 and 167.

_____

_____

_____

3 Give one fact and one opinion from the article about the people who actually built the Great Wall of China.

Hint

For clues, see pages 167 and 168.

_____

_____

_____

4 Why do you think the author ends the article with a series of opinions about visiting the Great Wall?

Hint

For clues, see page 170.

_____

_____

_____

abandon
bitterly
fury
massive
steadfast

Myths

① Every culture has its own myths, or legends. Myths explain things in nature or events in the history of a people. Characters are usually heroes, animals, or larger-than-life gods and goddesses. There may be no proof that a myth is true, but people may have a **steadfast** belief that it is!

Which of your friends do you think is the most steadfast? Explain.

_____

_____

_____

Zeus, the god of sky and thunder, was the most powerful Greek god.

② Dragons appear in many myths around the world. England's most famous myth, written almost a thousand years ago, is about a hero named Beowulf. He fought against the **fury** of a dragon.

Have you ever faced the fury of a storm? Explain.

_____

_____

_____

3 The myth of El Dorado, the City of Gold, has been told in South America since the 1500s. Explorers believed it was true. They searched for the gold but never found it. Today, people still dream of finding El Dorado. Nothing can make them **abandon** their dreams.

What might make someone <u>abandon</u> the idea of having a picnic in a park?

_____

_____

_____

4 A famous American myth is about a **massive** hero called Paul Bunyan. He was known for his strength and his huge sidekick, Babe the Blue Ox. They say Paul dug out the Great Lakes to provide water bowls for Babe!

Write a synonym for <u>massive</u>.

_____

5 The word "myth" is from the Greek word *mythos,* meaning "story." Greek myths are about gods and goddesses, heroes, and some **bitterly** fought wars. The oldest known Greek myths, dating from before 1200 B.C.E., are about events that took place during the ten-year-long Trojan War.

Why might people argue <u>bitterly</u> about music?

_____

_____

_____

A Gift for Troy

by Shirley Granahan

A famous Greek myth takes place in the ancient city of Troy. Some people think it's just a made-up story. Others believe it's based on real people and events.

Once upon a time, the city of Troy stood on the coast of what is now Turkey. In ancient times, people built walls around their cities to keep out their enemies. Troy had such a wall. It was very strong and high. The citizens of the city, Trojans, had a **steadfast** belief. They thought that as long as the wall stood, they would be safe inside the city.

Stop Think Write

STORY STRUCTURE

What is the setting for this part of the story?

_____

_____

_____

Troy was located across the sea from ancient Greece. The young prince of Troy, named Paris, sailed across the sea to Sparta, which was part of Greece. There he met Menelaus, the king of Sparta, and his wife, Helen.

Paris thought Helen was the most beautiful woman he had ever seen. While Menelaus was away, Paris kidnapped Helen and took her back to Troy.

Menelaus could not control his **fury** when he discovered what had happened. He wanted to kill Paris and free Helen, so he started a terrible war between Greece and Troy. It lasted for ten years.

Menelaus gathered soldiers from all over Greece. His brother, King Agamemnon, took command of the troops. They sailed to Troy to fight Paris and rescue Helen.

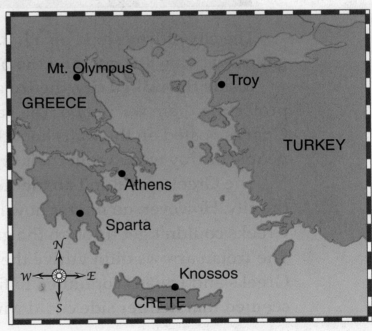

Stop | Think | Write

VOCABULARY

What happened as a result of Menelaus's <u>fury</u>?

_____

_____

_____

The city of Troy stood on a hill. The Greek army gathered below the city, and the battle began.

Inside the walled city, the Trojans felt safe. The walls protecting them were solid. The gates were locked. Guards posted on the walls kept the Greeks out, so the people of Troy went about their everyday lives.

The Greeks wouldn't **abandon** their fight to destroy the city. However, no matter how hard they tried, the Greeks couldn't get through the gates or over the walls. The Trojan arrows didn't drive the Greeks away, so the Greeks and Trojans continued to fight year after year. It seemed that neither side could win.

Stop Think Write

What is the problem in this part of the story?

_____

_____

_____

The Trojans had a special statue of the goddess Athena in a temple that was dedicated to her. Athena was the goddess of wisdom and war. The Trojans thought they could resist any enemy attack as long as they had that statue. However, two Greek soldiers were somehow able to sneak into the temple, steal the statue, and take it away. Some Trojans saw that as a sign that they would lose the war.

According to legend, the gods looked on while the Greeks and the Trojans fought. The gods even chose sides. Zeus, the father of all gods, wanted the Trojans to win. Athena, although loved by the Trojans, sided with the Greeks.

The goddess Athena was very clever and came up with a plan to help the Greeks defeat the Trojans.

Stop | Think | Write

STORY STRUCTURE

How did the theft of the statue change the feelings of some Trojans?

_____

_____

_____

Athena told the Greeks to build a **massive**, hollow wooden horse. When it was finished, the best Greek soldiers hid inside. The rest of the Greeks returned to their ships and sailed out of sight in the dark of night. Before they left, they rolled the horse to the gates of Troy.

The next morning, the Trojans saw that the Greeks were gone. They thought the war was over and they had won! Then they discovered the huge horse outside the city gates. The Trojan people thought the wooden horse was a gift or a sign of peace. They decided to move it inside the city.

"Don't do it!" a few Trojans warned. "Beware of Greeks bearing gifts!" The other citizens refused to listen.

Stop | Think | Write

VOCABULARY

Why did the wooden horse need to be <u>massive</u>?

_____

_____

_____

The horse was too big to go through the gates. Stone by stone, the Trojans tore down part of the wall to get the horse inside. They rolled it to a spot near the temple of Athena. Then they had a big party to celebrate winning the war.

That night, the Greek ships silently returned to Troy. In the early morning, the Greek soldiers climbed out of the horse. They surprised and attacked the Trojan guards. Then the rest of the Greek army stormed into the city.

The Greeks **bitterly** attacked the Trojans. All the Trojan men, including Paris, were killed. All the Trojan women were sent to Greece as slaves. Helen was rescued, and the city of Troy was burned to the ground. At last, the long war was over.

Stop | Think | Write

STORY STRUCTURE

How was King Menelaus's conflict resolved?

_____

_____

_____

Today, people still tell the story of the giant wooden horse that helped to end a ten-year war. Is the story of the Trojan horse true? Archaeologists have found the story written in ancient books. Also, the horse and scenes from the battle are found in ancient art discovered in the area. Still, some people think that evidence shows only that the Trojan horse was a good story. They don't believe it proves that the events actually took place. Only the people of ancient Greece and Troy know for sure . . . and they're not talking.

Stop Think Write

What have archaeologists found that could indicate that this myth is true?

_____

_____

_____

Look Back and Respond

1 Who was Paris?

_____

_____

_____

Hint

For a clue, see page 175.

2 Why did King Agamemnon sail to Troy with Greek troops?

_____

_____

_____

Hint

For a clue, see page 175.

3 How did the Trojans get the massive horse through the gate?

_____

_____

_____

Hint

For a clue, see page 179.

4 How might archaeologists finally prove that the Trojan horse was real?

_____

_____

_____

Hint

Think about evidence you would need to convince you.

Lesson
19

✓ **TARGET VOCABULARY**

ceremonial
divine
erected
fragments
pondered

Ancient Cultures

Check the answer.

1 Every culture has its _____ objects. These are items that are used at events like births, weddings, deaths, and the appointment of new rulers. Each object has a special purpose and meaning.

☐ pondered ☐ erected ☐ ceremonial

2 In some ancient cultures, people believed that their rulers were _____. The ruler was thought to be more like a god than like an ordinary person.

☐ divine ☐ ceremonial ☐ lustrous

3 In every age, people have _____ monuments and statues. We build these things to honor a person or to remember an important event in history. For example, the Great Pyramids of Egypt were raised as tombs for ancient Egyptian kings.

☐ affirmed ☐ erected ☐ divine

4 Very few objects survive over the centuries. Pottery and stone tools are often in _____ when they are discovered. We can study these small pieces, try to put them back together, and guess how they were first used.

☐ **fragments**   ☐ **ceremonial**   ☐ **agony**

5 For years, experts have _____ questions about vanished civilizations. What became of these people of the past? Scientists and historians think long and hard about ways of life that have disappeared.

☐ **pondered**   ☐ **erected**   ☐ **sacrificed**

6 Describe a <u>ceremonial</u> object that you have seen. How was it used?

_____

_____

7 Describe a statue or monument that was <u>erected</u> in your city, town, or state.

_____

_____

8 What kinds of objects might break into <u>fragments</u>?

_____

_____

Finding King Tut

by Carol Alexander

It was a November afternoon in 1922. Howard Carter stood scanning the dunes in the Valley of the Kings. He and his team had come to Egypt to look for the resting place of King Tut, an Egyptian king of long ago. The ancient Egyptians had **erected** huge pyramids for some dead rulers. Others were buried in elaborate underground tombs. Carter thought the tomb of King Tut might lay buried under the drifting sand.

Carter had spent four years digging in this valley. A wealthy Englishman, Lord Carnarvon, was funding the work. However, Carter's team was running out of time. Lord Carnarvon had given them one last season to find the tomb of King Tut. Then the money would run out.

Stop | Think | Write

CAUSE AND EFFECT

Why might Howard Carter have to abandon his search for King Tut's tomb?

_____

_____

_____

From Artist to Explorer

Howard Carter was born in England in 1874. As a boy, he learned to draw and paint. His father, an artist, trained him. In 1899, Howard Carter met Percy Edward Newberry. Newberry belonged to the Egypt Exploration Fund, and he needed an artist to join his dig. He hired Carter to copy the drawings and symbols on Egyptian tombs and objects.

Carter copied scenes from the walls of tombs, and he quickly became skilled at his work. Later, he landed a place on a team of scientists led by the famous archaeologist William Petrie. At first, Petrie did not think young Carter was experienced enough to join his team.

Carter proved Petrie wrong. He quickly learned all he had to know to do a good job. With Petrie for a teacher, Carter gained knowledge and experience. He became a leading explorer of Egypt's past.

Stop | Think | Write

CAUSE AND EFFECT

How did Carter's training as an artist qualify him to join Percy Edward Newberry's dig?

_____

_____

_____

Journey to the Valley of the Kings

In 1908, Howard Carter met Lord Carnarvon, who owned a valuable collection of Egyptian artifacts. Lord Carnarvon wanted to find the tomb of an Egyptian king who was little known at that time, Tutankhamen. Carter was hired to lead the dig.

Howard Carter's team began working in earnest in 1917. Carter was prepared to dig down to the bedrock to find the tomb. However, after five years, his team had little to show for their work except a few artifacts bearing the dead king's name.

As Carter looked out over the Valley of the Kings on that November afternoon, he must have **pondered** the fate of the dig. After all their hard work, would they have to abandon the project? A young man ran toward Carter. Usually, this worker carried water for the team. He told Carter that he had come across a stone step while going about his work. He thought Carter would want to know about this right away.

Stop | Think | Write

CAUSE AND EFFECT

Why did the water bearer run to Carter?

_____

_____

_____

Carter followed the boy to the stone step and began digging around it. More steps led downward. Carter was thrilled to think that at last they might have found the entrance to the ancient king's tomb.

Three days later, the crew had dug all the way down to a sealed door. There were royal seals on the door, but Carter could not read them. He found evidence that ancient tomb raiders had broken a small hole through the door. Surely, the raiders couldn't have taken much through the small hole. Carter wondered if his team would find the tomb intact when they opened it.

Carter had to wait before learning the answer to his question. He contacted Lord Carnarvon and told him of their discovery. He knew that Lord Carnarvon and his daughter, Lady Herbert, would want to be present at the moment when they first entered the tomb.

Stop Think Write

CAUSE AND EFFECT

Why didn't Carter unseal and enter the tomb right away?

_____

_____

_____

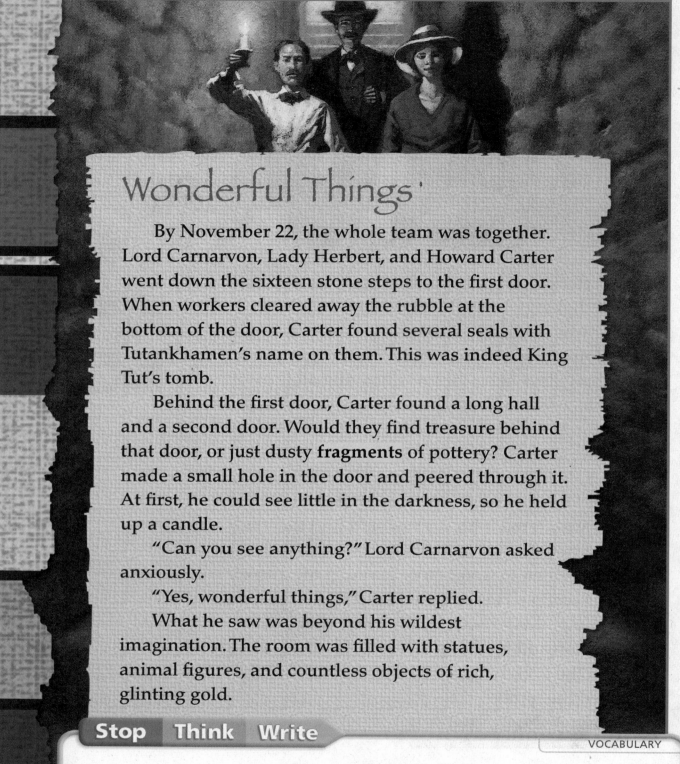

Wonderful Things

By November 22, the whole team was together. Lord Carnarvon, Lady Herbert, and Howard Carter went down the sixteen stone steps to the first door. When workers cleared away the rubble at the bottom of the door, Carter found several seals with Tutankhamen's name on them. This was indeed King Tut's tomb.

Behind the first door, Carter found a long hall and a second door. Would they find treasure behind that door, or just dusty **fragments** of pottery? Carter made a small hole in the door and peered through it. At first, he could see little in the darkness, so he held up a candle.

"Can you see anything?" Lord Carnarvon asked anxiously.

"Yes, wonderful things," Carter replied.

What he saw was beyond his wildest imagination. The room was filled with statues, animal figures, and countless objects of rich, glinting gold.

Stop Think Write

Why might Carter have expected objects in the tomb to be in **fragments**?

_____

_____

_____

Over the next days, weeks, and months, Carter's team worked slowly and carefully to examine the chambers of King Tut's tomb. They found the king's mummy in a series of coffins, including one made of solid gold. They found many gems and works of art. They found **ceremonial** objects, including a throne and a gold mask. There were hundreds of precious items.

The Egyptians believed their kings were **divine**, so they buried them with great care. Many rich objects were placed in the burial chambers of the kings. The Egyptians believed that these things would be used in the afterlife. King Tut was buried with all of his wealth.

The items in King Tut's tomb were over three thousand years old. Carter knew that people all over the world would want to see these works of art. Scientists would be interested in King Tut's mummy, too. People would be studying findings from the tomb for many years to come. Many of the treasures would end up in museums.

| Stop | Think | Write |

VOCABULARY

How might the <u>ceremonial</u> objects in King Tut's tomb have been used?

_____

_____

_____

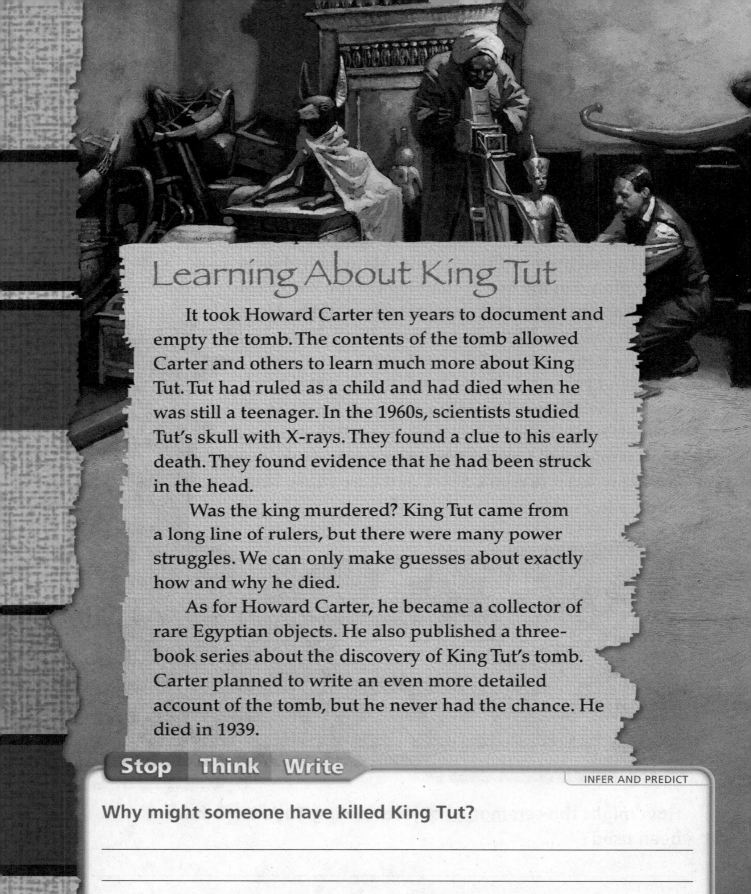

Learning About King Tut

It took Howard Carter ten years to document and empty the tomb. The contents of the tomb allowed Carter and others to learn much more about King Tut. Tut had ruled as a child and had died when he was still a teenager. In the 1960s, scientists studied Tut's skull with X-rays. They found a clue to his early death. They found evidence that he had been struck in the head.

Was the king murdered? King Tut came from a long line of rulers, but there were many power struggles. We can only make guesses about exactly how and why he died.

As for Howard Carter, he became a collector of rare Egyptian objects. He also published a three-book series about the discovery of King Tut's tomb. Carter planned to write an even more detailed account of the tomb, but he never had the chance. He died in 1939.

Stop **Think** **Write**

INFER AND PREDICT

Why might someone have killed King Tut?

_____

_____

_____

Look Back and Respond

1 Why was it important for Egyptian explorers to have an artist along on digs?

_____

_____

_____

Hint

For clues, see page 185.

2 Why did Carter's team have to work slowly and carefully to examine King Tut's tomb?

_____

_____

_____

Hint

For a clue, see page 189.

3 Why did the Egyptians bury their rulers in grand tombs filled with valuable objects?

_____

_____

_____

Hint

For a clue, see page 189.

4 Do you think Howard Carter was a great archaeologist and explorer? Explain.

_____

_____

Hint

Clues you can use are on almost every page!

meager
opulent
salvage
subjected
tremors

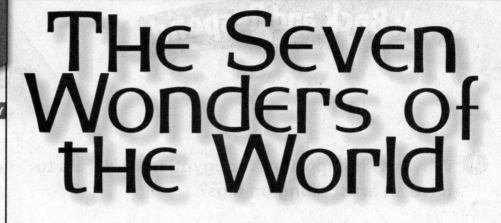

The Seven Wonders of the World

People have always traveled the world to see remarkable structures made by man. In ancient times, historians and scholars made lists of places that were especially large, unusual, or **(1)** _____. One such list was called the Seven Wonders of the World. The Seven Wonders of the World were the Great Pyramid of Giza, the Colossus of Rhodes, the Hanging Gardens of Babylon, the Lighthouse of Alexandria, the Statue of Zeus at Olympia, the Temple of Artemis at Ephesus, and the Mausoleum at Halicarnassus.

The Seven Wonders of the World were grand and beautiful, but many people who built them had hard lives. Many workers were slaves or laborers who earned **2** _____ wages. Workers were often **3** _____ to harsh conditions. There were no cranes or bulldozers in ancient times. Workers had to haul huge slabs of stone and lift them into place by hand.

Only one of the Seven Wonders of the World still exists today: the Great Pyramid of Giza. Some structures collapsed due to the **4** _____ of powerful earthquakes. Other structures were destroyed by fires. People may have tried to **5** _____ these amazing structures. However, little or nothing remains of them today.

THE SECRETS OF AN ANCIENT STATUE

by John Berry

Have you ever seen the Statue of Liberty? This famous statue stands proud in New York Harbor. A gift from France to the United States, the statue is a symbol of freedom.

Two thousand years before the Statue of Liberty, there was another great statue called the Colossus of Rhodes. It stood on land that is now part of Turkey. The Colossus no longer exists. It was destroyed less than six decades after it was built.

The story of the Colossus of Rhodes is important because it helps reveal what life was like in ancient times. Who lived in the region? What did people do for a living? Why did they build the statue?

Rhodes is an island off the coast of Turkey. In ancient times, the people were farmers. Their land was fertile and they grew many crops. They believed that the Greek sun god, Helios, blessed them.

Stop **Think** **Write**

MAIN IDEAS AND DETAILS

Why is the story of the Colossus of Rhodes important?

_____

_____

_____

A Long, Difficult War

The inhabitants of Rhodes were peaceful people, but they did have enemies. The enemies wanted to control their rich land and thriving port. They hoped to collect taxes from the people of Rhodes.

In 305 B.C.E., Greek soldiers attacked Rhodes. The people bravely fought back. The year-long battle resulted in many deaths. Farmland went untended, and many people had only **meager** supplies of food. The people were hungry and desperate, but they were determined to protect their homes. Finally, the Greek soldiers gave up, abandoning much of their war equipment as they fled.

The people of Rhodes were thankful. They believed that Helios helped them win the war. They decided to build a giant statue to honor the sun god. The statue would be called the Colossus of Rhodes.

Stop Think Write

MAIN IDEAS AND DETAILS

What detail supports the idea that the people of Rhodes were thankful for the outcome of the war?

_____

_____

_____

Building the Colossus of Rhodes

To this day, how the people got the materials to build the Colossus of Rhodes remains a mystery. Many people believe that the citizens of Rhodes decided to **salvage** war equipment left behind by the Greeks. The people of Rhodes might have sold the Greek war equipment and used the money to buy the materials for the statue. Another possibility is that people melted the bronze swords and shields and used the metal to build the statue.

There are no photographs of the statue because it was built long before the invention of the camera. As a result, no one knows exactly what it looked like. However, ancient records tell us a man named Chares designed the Colossus of Rhodes and that it stood about 110 feet tall. That's as high as an eleven-story building!

Stop | **Think** | **Write**

VOCABULARY

What are two possible ways the people of Rhodes might have used the Greek war equipment that they were able to salvage?

_____

_____

_____

Completing the Colossus

The Colossus was golden, a perfect color for honoring the sun god. Workers shaped the bronze into hollow sections and placed each new section on top of the last one. Slowly, the statue rose from the ground. To reach each part, workers stood on mounds of dirt.

Builders put stones and iron bars inside the sections to support the statue and to ensure that it would not tip over. Workers built the head of the statue last. Many believe the face looked like that of Alexander the Great, a world leader before the statue was built. To honor Helios, the statue probably wore a crown with long points that looked like the rays of the sun.

After twelve years of building, the giant, **opulent** statue was finally completed in about 282 B.C.E.

Stop | Think | Write

CAUSE AND EFFECT

Why did the workers put stones and iron bars inside the statue?

_____

_____

_____

The Colossus Falls

The people of Rhodes were very proud of the Colossus. They thought it would stand for thousands of years.

Sadly, the bronze giant didn't stay intact that long. In 226 B.C.E., less than sixty years after it was built, a strong earthquake struck Rhodes. **Tremors** caused the statue to snap apart at the knees. It fell to the ground, shattering into pieces.

Many people wanted to fix the statue, including the ruler of Egypt. He even offered to pay the cost of rebuilding. Not sure what to do, the people of Rhodes asked the advice of a wise person. He told them not to rebuild the statue. He said the statue fell because the gods were unhappy. The people listened, and left the great statue on the ground.

The broken Colossus drew crowds. Up close, it seemed even larger than before. People tried to wrap their arms around the huge fingers. One ancient writer wrote, "Few people can make their arms meet around the thumb of the figure."

Stop Think Write

VOCABULARY

What effect did earthquake tremors have on the Colossus of Rhodes?

_____

_____

_____

A Cycle of War

The broken statue remained on the ground for nearly 900 years. In 654 C.E., war came to Rhodes again. The people were defeated this time.

A Syrian prince took control of Rhodes and **subjected** the people of Rhodes to his rule. He ordered his soldiers to take apart the Colossus. They packed the bronze pieces onto camels that carried the heavy loads to ships. Some say it took 900 camels to carry away all that metal. The ships sailed to the mainland. From there the bronze was hauled to Syria.

What happened to the bronze in Syria? Some think it was melted down to make coins. Others believe it was melted and turned back into swords and shields, since that was the fate of many old statues of the time. Perhaps the Colossus began and ended as war equipment, something the people of Rhodes wouldn't have wanted.

Stop Think Write

MAIN IDEAS AND DETAILS

What are two possible reasons that the Syrian prince ordered the pieces of the Colossus to be taken to Syria?

_____

_____

_____

The Mystery Remains

We know many facts about the Colossus of Rhodes, but some details remain a mystery. For example, where did the statue stand? An artist drew a famous picture in the 1500s of the Colossus standing at the entrance to the harbor with its feet spread far apart for ships to pass through.

Today we know that this cannot be true. Scientists explain that the legs couldn't have been spread apart because the statue was too heavy and would not have stayed standing.

Many scholars think its feet were closer together, and that one arm may have been raised. The Colossus may have held a bowl of fire, or a lit torch, in which case, it really would have resembled the Statue of Liberty.

One thing is sure, though. The Colossus was so great that it gave us new words. The word *colossus* means "a giant statue." The word *colossal* means "amazingly huge."

Stop | **Think** | **Write**

MAIN IDEAS AND DETAILS

What details help scholars conclude that the Colossus could not have had its legs spread apart?

_____

_____

_____

Look Back and Respond

1 What are some things about the Colossus of Rhodes that made it a "great" statue?

_____

_____

Hint

Look for clues on pages 195, 196, 197, and 198.

2 How did wars play a part in the story of the Colossus of Rhodes?

_____

_____

Hint

For clues, see pages 195, 196, and 199.

3 How did the workers build such a huge statue?

_____

_____

Hint

Look for a clue on page 197.

4 Why didn't the people rebuild the Colossus after it fell?

_____

_____

Hint

Look for a clue on page 198.

abrupt
blurted
eventually
jeopardy
spiteful

Friendship

1 "That new girl Beth is weird!" Lucy **blurted** to her friend Mara. She had forgotten that Mara was Beth's cousin.

Think of a time you <u>blurted</u> out something and then felt bad about it. Tell what happened.

_____

_____

_____

2 Mara suddenly stopped talking to Lucy. Lucy did not understand Mara's **abrupt** behavior.

Write an antonym for the word <u>abrupt</u>.

_____

3 Lucy could tell her friendship with Mara was in **jeopardy**. If the girls could not work out their differences, their friendship was in danger of ending.

Why is Lucy and Mara's friendship in <u>jeopardy</u>?

_____

_____

_____

4 Lucy could not remember doing anything **spiteful** to Mara. Lucy had not said anything on purpose to hurt Mara or make her angry.

Describe a time someone did something <u>spiteful</u> to you.

_____

_____

_____

5 **Eventually**, Lucy asked Mara why she was angry. When Lucy realized what she had done, she felt terrible.

If you are not nice to a friend, what might <u>eventually</u> happen to the friendship?

_____

_____

_____

Everyone's Favorite Music

by Mia Lewis

Jay Kovak and Julio Santiago lived in a neighborhood with people of all different races and nationalities. People spoke English, but you could also hear Chinese, Portuguese, Russian, Creole, Laotian, and more than one kind of Spanish.

Every summer, the neighbors had a big party. There was always lots of food, fun, and music! Neighbors took turns hosting the party. This summer it was the Santiago family's turn.

Julio was excited. His mom put him in charge of the music. Last year, the Kovaks hosted the party. Jay had planned the music, with Julio's help of course.

Jay and Julio had been best friends since they were in preschool. Now they were in the same sixth-grade class, and still best friends. Julio had a new friend named Eli Jones. Julio was planning to ask Eli to help with the music, too.

Stop Think Write

COMPARE AND CONTRAST

How is the preparation for this year's party different from last year?

_____

_____

_____

Mrs. Santiago was concerned about the boys' choice of music. "The music is supposed to *entertain* people," she reminded them. "It should make them sing and dance. The music is for *everyone*."

"Don't worry, Mami," said Julio. "This party is going to be the best ever! The three of us will have fun working together. Right, Jay? Right, Eli?"

"Right!" said Eli. "I know all the hottest hits. Leave it to me, Mrs. Santiago."

Jay said nothing. He didn't think it would be fun working with Eli. Eli didn't even live in the neighborhood.

Mrs. Santiago could sense Jay's concern. She worried that three boys might be one too many for this project. She hoped Julio's friendship with Jay wasn't in **jeopardy**.

Stop   Think   Write

COMPARE AND CONTRAST

How does Julio feel about the three boys working together? How does Jay feel?

_____

_____

_____

"Let's have lots of Latin music because it's best for dancing," announced Julio, as the three began planning.

"Latin music is great," agreed Jay. "The neighbors loved that music from last year's party. And let's include some R & B favorites for our parents."

"Are you guys kidding?" asked Eli. "We don't want that old stuff! We've got to play what's hot—the hip-hop songs from the top of the charts."

"Who asked you?" **blurted** out Jay. "Our neighbors don't like that kind of music!"

Jay was not a **spiteful** person, but he didn't like Eli's I-know-best attitude. It bothered him that Julio was letting Eli have a say in their party. He wished it were just him and Julio planning the music, like last year.

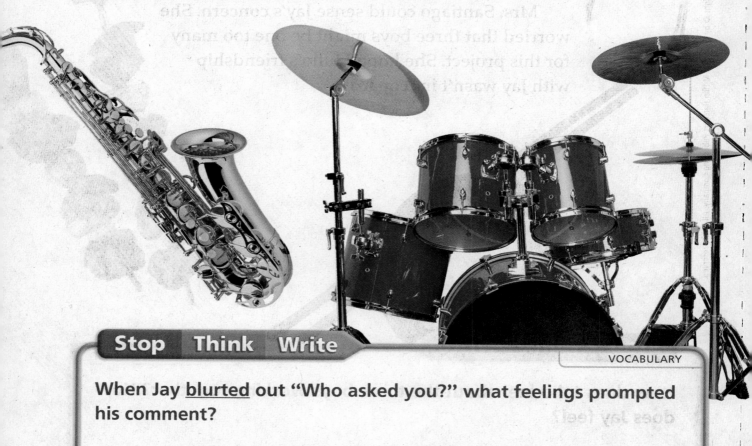

Stop | Think | Write

When Jay **blurted** out "Who asked you?" what feelings prompted his comment?

_____

_____

_____

"Hold on," said Julio calmly. "There's no need to get mad. Lots of people enjoy hip-hop, Jay. That's why it's at the top of the charts, buddy! Even *I* like it!"

"That's right!" said Eli, sounding proud of himself, like he was the winner of a competition. "Everything changes, you know."

"But Eli, I like Latin music too, and my mom likes R & B," said Julio. "Lots of different people are coming to this party, so we should have music for everyone—disco, funk, mambo, country, R & B, *and* rap. Our neighborhood is all about diversity."

"Yeah," said Jay, nodding in agreement at Julio's idea. "Our neighborhood is a mix of all types! We have to play a mix of music that *all* of our neighbors will enjoy."

Stop | Think | Write

COMPARE AND CONTRAST

Compare and contrast Eli's ideas about music for the party on pages 206 and 207, with Julio's and Jay's ideas.

_____

_____

_____

207

Eli was quiet for a while, and he looked like he was thinking hard. **Eventually** he spoke.

"You guys are right," said Eli. "The music is not about what's hot. It's about what people like. Don't forget what Julio's mom said. The music should get *everyone* dancing and singing. How do we know what kind of dance music everyone likes, though? Maybe there's Chinese dance music we don't know about. Or Brazilian. Also, what about that grumpy guy who lives on the corner? What kind of music do you think *he* likes?"

Jay smiled. Eli was talking about Mr. Bromley. He always sat on his front porch, frowning at everyone who passed by. He greeted kids by barking an **abrupt** warning: "You kids stay off my grass!" If Eli had noticed Mr. Bromley, maybe he was getting to know the neighborhood better than Jay had thought!

Stop | Think | Write

In the last paragraph, why is Mr. Bromley's greeting described as abrupt?

_____

_____

_____

"It's kind of you to think of Mr. Bromley," said Julio, "but let's face it. There's no way we can include the favorite music of every single person in the neighborhood."

"True," said Jay, "but I agree that it's a nice idea."

"It's more than an idea," said Eli with a smile. "If we work together, we can make it happen!"

Eli had a plan. The boys would ask each neighbor for a recording of his or her favorite music. Then they would make a compilation! The final CD would really be *everyone's* favorite music!

Jay had to admit that Eli's idea was brilliant. Eli had been willing to change his mind about what music to play. Maybe it was time for Jay to change his mind about Eli.

Stop   Think   Write

INFER AND PREDICT

Why does Jay think Eli's idea is brilliant?

_____

_____

_____

The boys carried out Eli's plan. They went from house to house, gathering music. By the time they finished, they had collected fifty-year-old records, twenty-five-year-old tapes, CDs, and digital files on flash drives. The music was a true mix of generations and nationalities.

Jay enjoyed listening to the different music. He even liked working with Eli. He was beginning to see why Julio was friends with him.

That year, the neighborhood party was hot in every way. The July sun was hot. The food was hot and spicy, thanks to Mami's Latin cooking. Most of all, the dance music was hot, hot, hot!

Everyone danced, even Mr. Bromley.

Stop **Think** **Write**

COMPARE AND CONTRAST

How does the music at this year's party differ from the music in previous years?

_____

_____

Look Back and Respond

1 Mrs. Santiago is worried about two things at the beginning of the story. What are they?

_____

_____

_____

Hint

For clues, look on page 205.

2 At first, what kind of music do Julio and Jay think they should play at the party? How does this compare to what Eli thinks?

_____

_____

_____

Hint

For clues, see page 206.

3 How does Eli's idea for party music change? Why does it change?

_____

_____

_____

Hint

For clues, see pages 207 and 208.

4 Compare and contrast how Jay feels about Eli at the beginning and at the end of the story.

_____

_____

_____

Hint

For clues, see pages 205, 206, 208, and 209.

✓ **TARGET VOCABULARY**

**conditions
decrepit
frustration
harsh
instinct**

Early Attempts to Fly

1 A bird knows how to fly by **instinct**. It is born knowing how to flap its wings. Flying comes naturally for a bird.

Describe something else an animal might do by instinct.

_____

_____

_____

2 Throughout history, people have dreamed of flying. Early efforts were met with **frustration**. The first flying machines did not work very well.

What causes you frustration?

_____

_____

_____

3 Some early inventors made aircraft from very light materials that would float on the air currents. These aircraft often fell apart in strong, **harsh** winds.

Write an antonym for <u>harsh</u>.

_____

4 Inventors looked for places with perfect **conditions** to test their aircraft. The wind speed and direction had to be just right to lift the aircraft off the ground.

What are the best <u>conditions</u> for doing homework?

_____

_____

_____

5 Aircraft can become worn and **decrepit** over time. They might fall apart completely if they aren't carefully maintained.

What else can become <u>decrepit</u> over time? Why?

_____

Amelia Earhart
Pioneer Pilot

by K.C. Archer

Amelia Earhart was a pioneer who changed how people thought about flying and pilots. She changed how people thought about what women can do.

Amelia Earhart was born on July 24, 1897. She saw her first plane at a state fair when she was ten years old. She was not impressed by the rusty and **decrepit** aircraft.

When she was twenty, Amelia went to a stunt-flying show with a friend. The pilots performed tricks in their airplanes. A pilot saw Amelia and her friend, and he tried to scare the women by flying straight at them. Amelia did not move an inch.

Instead of being afraid, Amelia was fascinated. She knew then that flying was her future.

Stop Think Write

VOCABULARY

What might a decrepit aircraft look like?

_____

_____

_____

Young Amelia

Friends were not surprised by Amelia's interest in planes. Amelia was always looking for adventure, and she liked to do things that were off-limits for women at that time. She kept a scrapbook of articles about pioneering women. Most of the articles were about women in engineering, law, and other male-dominated fields. Amelia knew that women were just as smart and capable as men were. She wanted to prove this to the world.

Amelia graduated from high school in 1915. She worked as a nurse's aid in Canada during World War I, taking care of wounded soldiers. Later, she went to college and then got a job as a social worker. She began to save money.

Stop | Think | Write

CONCLUSIONS AND GENERALIZATIONS

What details help you conclude that Amelia Earhart was different from most women of her time?

_____

_____

_____

Flying the *Canary*

January 3, 1921 was a day that changed Amelia's life forever. On that day she had her first flying lesson. Amelia loved to fly and learned quickly. She had an **instinct** for flying.

Six months after she began flying, Amelia bought her own plane. It was small and yellow and fit only two people. She called it *Canary*.

In October of 1922, Amelia flew 14,000 feet high in her plane. It was the first time a woman had flown that high! Already Amelia was breaking records, but rather than joy, she felt **frustration**. She had set a world record, but no one paid attention. Although the world didn't think of her as a great pilot, Amelia didn't give up. She kept her job as a social worker and flew her plane as a hobby. Her big break came a few years later.

Stop **Think** **Write**

CONCLUSIONS AND GENERALIZATIONS

Why didn't the world think of Amelia Earhart as a great pilot?

_____

_____

_____

A Dream Come True

In 1928, Amelia got a phone call from a man who asked if she would like to fly across the Atlantic Ocean. Amelia was thrilled, but she wondered if the call was a trick. Why would anyone ask *her* to fly on such a dangerous and important mission?

Amelia learned that the call was real and said yes. She went to New York and met the people who would fly across the Atlantic with her. Her copilot, Wilmer "Bill" Stultz, was well-known and respected. Louis E. "Slim" Gordon would be onboard as the mechanic. His job was to fix anything that went wrong with the plane during the flight.

Stop **Think** **Write**

CONCLUSIONS AND GENERALIZATIONS

Why might Amelia Earhart have thought the phone call was not real?

_____

_____

_____

A World-Famous Journey

On June 17, 1928, Amelia, Bill, and Slim took off from the east coast of Canada. They flew a small plane called *Friendship*. The plane was faster than other airplanes of the time. Even so, it took almost twenty-one hours to reach Great Britain. The journey was long and difficult, and **conditions** on the little plane were **harsh**. Amelia and her crew flew through fog and lightning and were blown off course by strong winds.

When they arrived in Great Britain, Amelia, Bill, and Slim were instantly famous. People around the world heard the story of their journey. At last, Amelia received recognition for her daring and skill.

Amelia was happy, but she wanted to do more. She decided to spend her time setting new world records. From then on, the sky was the limit.

Stop	Think	Write

VOCABULARY

What was harsh about the flight across the Atlantic?

_____

_____

_____

Breaking Records

In 1929, Amelia joined the National Aeronautic Association. She wanted to create separate flying records for women. She set and broke many of those records herself, including the record for fastest speed in an airplane.

In 1932, Amelia made a second journey across the Atlantic. This time she traveled alone. She was the first woman to fly solo across the Atlantic Ocean. The trip took just fourteen hours and fifty-six minutes.

Later that year, Amelia set a record for speed. She flew across the United States in nineteen hours and five minutes. In 1933, she repeated the flight, breaking her own record for time. Two years later, Amelia flew more than 2,400 miles from California to Hawaii. There was no stopping her.

People's shock at her daring feats made Amelia push even harder. She was always ready for new and exciting challenges.

Stop **Think** **Write**

CAUSE AND EFFECT

What caused Amelia Earhart to try even harder to break records?

_____

_____

_____

What Happened to Amelia Earhart?

When Amelia Earhart was nearly forty years old, she decided to fly around the world. This journey would be her most dangerous yet.

Her flight began in Florida. For a month, Amelia flew east. She stopped in Africa, India, and finally, Papua, New Guinea.

The last part of the journey was across the Pacific Ocean. During the flight, Amelia lost touch with the U.S. Coast Guard. Her plane disappeared. A rescue mission searched for Amelia day after day. They found nothing.

To this day, no one knows for sure what happened.

Amelia Earhart is remembered as a woman who changed the world. She was a true pioneer of aviation.

Stop | **Think** | **Write**

UNDERSTANDING CHARACTERS

What made Amelia Earhart a pioneer?

_____

_____

_____

Look Back and Respond

1 Flying was a dangerous occupation when Amelia Earhart was young. Why weren't friends surprised that she was interested in flying?

Hint

For clues, see page 215.

_____

_____

_____

2 Why did Amelia Earhart like the challenge of setting and breaking records?

Hint

For clues, see pages 214, 215, 216, 218, and 219.

_____

_____

_____

3 Overall, how did Amelia Earhart live her life?

Hint

Clues are on almost every page!

_____

_____

_____

4 In what ways do you think Amelia Earhart changed what people thought women could achieve?

Hint

Think about all the things Amelia Earhart did.

_____

_____

_____

Lesson 23

✓ **TARGET VOCABULARY**

contempt
exasperated
intently
scornfully
subsided

A TIME OF WAR

On December 7, 1941, Japanese planes attacked Pearl Harbor, Hawaii. America declared war on Japan, and then Germany declared war on the United States. America had entered World War II. American soldiers fought **intently** against the enemy.

Many Japanese Americans and German Americans lived in the United States. Some other Americans were suspicious and felt hatred and **contempt**. They acted **scornfully** toward Japanese Americans and German Americans. Some people feared that Japanese Americans might help Japan, so the government made Japanese Americans live in internment camps. There were no camps for German Americans.

Many Japanese Americans became **exasperated** with the cramped conditions and suspicion they had to endure. However, they had to stay in the camps until Japan surrendered, in 1945. Once fears **subsided**, the camps were closed.

1 Some fearful Americans acted

_____

towards Americans from Japan and Germany.

2 Japanese Americans became

_____ with conditions in

internment camps.

3 Camps for Japanese Americans closed when fears

_____ .

4 When you are determined to do something, you act <u>intently</u>. Describe the last time you acted intently. What were you doing?

_____

_____

_____

5 Why might a person feel <u>contempt</u> for another person?

_____

_____

_____

IT'S MY COUNTRY, Too

By Margaret Maugenest

Life was good for my family in 1941. We owned a small hotel in Los Angeles. My brother Joe was ten, and I was twelve. We were typical American children who did well in school and played with our friends. Joe liked baseball, and I took art classes.

My parents, Kenji and Izumi Natsumi, were born in Japan. They got married in their twenties, and then they moved to the United States. They worked at a factory and saved every penny. With the help of a bank loan, they bought the hotel.

We lived in a small house. My father worked hard at the hotel, and my mom took care of our home. Joe and I loved to be at the hotel, and we enjoyed meeting the many people who stayed there.

Stop Think Write

CAUSE AND EFFECT

What were the narrator's parents able to do because they had worked hard and saved?

_____

_____

_____

On December 7, 1941, our lives changed forever.

Joe and I were playing catch when our mother yelled to us, "Sue, Joe, come inside!" As we entered the house, we could hear the news on the radio. There had been an attack at Pearl Harbor, Hawaii. We knew the U.S. Navy had many ships there. "The United States has been attacked by the Japanese," said my mother. Joe and I looked at each other, not sure what to think.

The phone rang. It was my father. I overheard my mother talking and crying. We stayed in the house all day, listening to the radio and worrying.

The next day, Joe and I walked to school as usual. We ran into Joe's friend, Sam. Sam looked down. "My mom says I can't play with you anymore."

Stop Think Write

CAUSE AND EFFECT

Why did the narrator's mother tell Sue and Joe to come inside?

_____

_____

_____

Joe didn't understand why Sam said this. I thought, "It must be because of the Japanese bombing the ships. How can Sam's mom think we had anything to do with that? We're Americans. We were born here."

Before long, the United States entered World War II, fighting against Germany and Japan. Everyone was nervous and upset about the war. Some people looked at us with **contempt**, even though they had no reason to hate us. They treated us **scornfully**, as if we had done something horrible. It made me very sad.

In March 1942, my mother gave us some horrible news. The United States government was forcing Japanese Americans in some western states out of their homes. They worried that Japan was going to attack the West Coast and that Japanese people living there would help.

Stop Think Write

VOCABULARY

How might it feel if someone treated you with contempt even though you did nothing wrong?

_____

_____

_____

"Where are we supposed to go?" I asked.

"I don't know," my mother replied.

"How long will we be gone?" Joe wanted to know.

"No one knows," she responded sadly.

My mother and father discussed the situation with Japanese friends. They learned that there would be ten internment camps where Japanese Americans would be forced to live. We had only a few weeks to leave our homes and report to a camp.

Over the next three weeks, we sold most of our belongings—our car, furniture, books, and house. Father was forced to sell the hotel for a very low price. Our neighbor, Mrs. Daniels, let us store some things in her basement. Mostly we just kept clothing to wear at the camp. I never cried so much. My nice life was quickly becoming awful.

Stop | Think | Write

CAUSE AND EFFECT

Why did the family sell most of their belongings and the hotel?

_____

_____

_____

At the end of the month, we boarded a train to eastern California. We were assigned to a camp called Manzanar.

When we arrived there, guards searched and questioned us **intently**. We were assigned a tiny barrack to live in. Inside were small, straw mattresses. My father was furious, but he just sat down and said nothing.

A barbed-wire fence surrounded the camp. There were armed guards all around to make sure no one left. Over ten thousand Japanese Americans were living there. All of them were wondering why they were forced to live like this *in their own country*. They had done nothing wrong. Some people felt **exasperated** with the unfair situation.

I tried to write poems to make myself feel better. Months passed, and we managed, but I felt sad for the very little boys and girls forced to live in the camp.

Stop **Think** **Write**

UNDERSTANDING CHARACTERS

How did Sue feel about being in the Manzanar camp?

_____

_____

_____

By the spring of 1944, America was winning the war. Fear that Japanese Americans would help Japan **subsided**. At the start of 1945, the U.S. government announced that it would close the camps by the end of the year. All the people would be free to go.

We were happy, but worried. What would it be like when we returned home? How would other Americans treat us? Where would we live and what would we do? We had lost our house, our belongings, and the hotel.

In April 1945, we finally left Manzanar. Our old neighbor, Mrs. Daniels, picked us up at the train in Los Angeles. We were headed to Long Beach, where my uncle lived. He had been in a camp, too, but neighbors had taken care of his house. My family was going to stay with him until we were settled in our new lives.

Stop Think Write

VOCABULARY

What happened when the fear of Japanese Americans <u>subsided</u>?

_____

_____

_____

On our way to Long Beach, Joe asked, "Mrs. Daniels, will you drive us by our old house?"

My parents looked at each other. They wanted to see the house, but they also *didn't* want to see it. My father nodded to Mrs. Daniels, and we drove there.

Our street looked the same. We had sold the house to an older couple, and Mrs. Daniels said they had taken good care of it. Still, none of us could keep from feeling sad when we drove past it. I also felt anger, since my parents had worked so hard for that house, and they had lost it just because we were Japanese Americans.

At first, it was hard getting back to our old lives. Eventually life settled back to normal, at least a new normal. We would never forget our experience, but we had survived, and we were still together.

Stop Think Write

CAUSE AND EFFECT

Why did the narrator feel anger when she saw her old house?

_____

_____

_____

Look Back and Respond

1 Why did the U.S. government put Japanese Americans in internment camps?

_____

_____

_____

Hint

For a clue, see pages 226 and 227 of the story.

2 What effect did going to the camps have on the family in the story?

_____

_____

_____

Hint

For clues, see pages 227, 228, and 229 of the story.

3 How did seeing their old house make the family feel?

_____

_____

_____

Hint

For a clue, see page 230 of the story.

4 How can you tell that the writer's family had strength and courage?

_____

_____

_____

Hint

Clues you can use are on almost every page.

controversy
distinguished
inclined
prejudice
significance

The Supreme Court

The Supreme Court is the highest court in the United States. It is made up of nine

1 _____ judges,

or justices. The Supreme Court only hears very important cases that cannot be resolved in lower courts.

When people disagree about a law, they usually take their case to a local court to be resolved. If one side disagrees with the ruling of the local court, they may take the case to a higher court. There may be very strong arguments on both sides of a

2 _____. Even after local and state courts have ruled on a case, one side may not feel satisfied with the results.

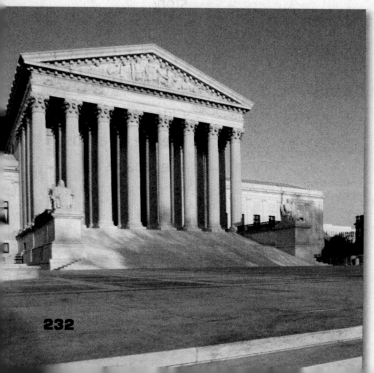

The Supreme Court Building, Washington, D.C.

The justices on the Supreme Court decide whether or not a case is important enough for them to hear. They only agree to hear cases of great

3 _____.

The Supreme Court has heard cases about

4 _____ toward people who felt that they were treated unfairly because of their gender, their religion, or the color of their skin.

After hearing both sides of a case, the justices of the Supreme Court may be

5 _____ to support one side or the other. They consider all of the arguments very carefully. They think long and hard about how national laws and the Constitution apply to the case. Then they vote. A decision by the Supreme Court overrules any decision made by lower courts.

Thurgood Marshall and Equal Rights

by Richard Stull

Sixty years ago, laws in some states were unfair to African Americans. The laws made sure that African Americans were segregated, or kept apart, from white people. African Americans could not eat in the same restaurants or sleep in the same hotels as white people. African Americans had to use different bathrooms in train stations and other public areas. They had to sit in the back of buses. Seats in the front were for white people.

The message was very clear: African Americans were to "stay in their place." The laws kept them unequal to white people.

Stop　Think　Write

AUTHOR'S PURPOSE

How does the author show that there was a need for African Americans to fight for equal rights?

_____

_____

_____

At that time, schools in some states were segregated, too. The law said that black students were not allowed to go to school with white students. African Americans went to their own schools. Schools for African Americans usually had less money for teachers and supplies than schools for white students.

That was what life was like when a case known as *Brown v. Board of Education* came before the Supreme Court.

The case began in Topeka, Kansas. Linda Brown was an African American third grader living in Topeka. She was not allowed to attend a white school that was close to her home. Instead, she had to ride a bus to a black school over a mile away.

In the fall of 1951, Linda Brown's father sued the Board of Education in Topeka. Twelve other parents facing the same problem joined Mr. Brown.

Stop **Think** **Write**

CAUSE AND EFFECT

Why did the parents of some African American students sue the Board of Education in Topeka?

_____

_____

_____

The NAACP Helps Out

The National Association for the Advancement of Colored People (NAACP) is a group that helps African Americans. The group believed that Linda Brown's case could be of great **significance** for black people. The NAACP decided to help Mr. Brown and the other parents. It assigned a lawyer named Thurgood Marshall to the case.

Marshall was born in 1908, and he grew up in Baltimore, Maryland. After high school, he went to Lincoln University—the nation's first African American college—and later to law school.

Marshall had fought for the rights of black people in the United States. He had won some important cases, including one that had gone to the Supreme Court. In that case, the court had decided that a Texas law was not fair to black voters.

The University of Maryland Law School, in Marshall's hometown of Baltimore, refused to admit Marshall because he was African American.

Stop | Think | Write

How would a ruling in favor of Brown be of great <u>significance</u> to black people?

_____

_____

_____

Marshall's Closing Argument

The Brown case went to the Supreme Court in 1952. Thurgood Marshall gave the final argument before the **distinguished** justices. "The only way to get equality," he said, "is for two people to get the same things, at the same place, and at the same time."

To support his argument, Marshall described the research of a doctor. The doctor had shown dolls to a group of African American students. One doll was black, and one was white. Most of the children said that the white doll was "good." They thought that the black doll was "bad."

Marshall argued that the experiment showed that the black students did not believe they were as good as white students. He believed the children felt this way because they were kept separate from white children.

Stop · Think · Write

MAIN IDEAS AND DETAILS

According to Marshall, what did the experiment with the dolls show about African American students?

_____

_____

_____

Marshall told the court that white and black kids played together all the time. They played after school. They played together in parks and on baseball fields.

He pointed out that the only place they were apart was in school. Marshall said that separating black and white children was just a way to make black children feel inferior, or less important. He described it as "America's sorry heritage from slavery."

Some of the Supreme Court justices were **inclined** to agree with Marshall. Others were not.

Should black and white children attend the same school or not? The court could not make up its mind about the **controversy**.

A classroom in a segregated elementary school

Stop Think Write

What was the <u>controversy</u> that Thurgood Marshall and the Topeka Board of Education argued about in the Supreme Court?

_____

_____

_____

A Historic Ruling

A few months later, Thurgood Marshall spoke in court again. This time, the nine justices agreed with Marshall. He won the case! On May 17, 1954, the Supreme Court ruled that segregation based on race was against the law.

The case made Thurgood Marshall a famous man. He became a judge on the U.S. Court of Appeals. After that, he became the first African American justice on the U.S. Supreme Court. He served twenty-four years. In that time, he fought for equal rights for African Americans. No one fought harder against **prejudice** than Thurgood Marshall.

Marshall (center) celebrates after the _Brown v. Board of Education_ ruling.

Marshall (left) marches for civil rights.

Stop Think Write

INFER AND PREDICT

How do you think Marshall's victory in _Brown v. Board of Education_ affected African American students?

_____

_____

_____

Before *Brown vs. Board of Education*

The year was 1930. Marshall wanted to go to law school. He tried to go to the University of Maryland. The school rejected him because he was black.

He went to Howard University Law School. He graduated at the top of his class and got a job as a lawyer with the NAACP.

Marshall argued a case for a black man named Donald Murray. Murray had applied to the University of Maryland Law School. Like Marshall, he was turned down because of his race.

The argument was that since Maryland had only one law school, it had failed to provide "separate but equal" educational opportunities for nonwhite students.

Marshall won the case. White judges ruled that the only way to give Murray an "equal" education was to admit him to the University of Maryland Law School.

Marshall (left) and Murray (center) prepare for court.

Stop Think Write

INFER AND PREDICT

Do you think that Marshall's commitment to equal rights was affected by his personal experiences? Explain.

_____

_____

_____

Look Back and Respond

1 Did the author write this selection to inform, persuade, or entertain readers? Explain.

_____

_____

_____

Hint

You can find clues on almost every page.

2 What were the main points Marshall made during the *Brown v. Board of Education* case?

_____

_____

_____

Hint

For clues, see pages 237 and 238.

3 What were some of Thurgood Marshall's main accomplishments?

_____

_____

_____

Hint

Clues appear on several pages. For example, see pages 236, 239, and 240.

4 What did Donald Murray and Thurgood Marshall have in common?

_____

_____

_____

Hint

For clues, see page page 240.

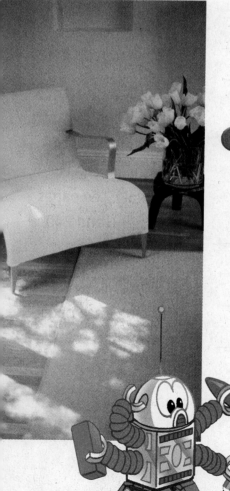

Lesson 25

✓ TARGET VOCABULARY

artificial
data
sensors
ultimate
uncanny

A New-Age Vacuum Cleaner

1 The Smiths' new vacuum cleaner is amazing. It has an **uncanny** ability to move around furniture without the help of a human being.

Describe a tool or a machine that you think has an uncanny ability to do something special.

_____

_____

_____

2 The vacuum cleaner has motion **sensors**. If they detect something that moves, like a cat, the vacuum cleaner turns away.

Imagine that you are building a flying machine. What kind of sensors would you put in it?

_____

_____

_____

3 A computer chip in the vacuum cleaner processes **data**. Some of the information comes from the sensors. The rest comes from the Smiths, who give the machine its instructions.

Describe an experiment that you conducted. What kind of <u>data</u> did you get?

_____

_____

_____

4 The vacuum cleaner has **artificial** intelligence. It can "think" and react, but it is not alive.

Tell about something <u>artificial</u> that you know about or have seen.

_____

_____

_____

5 Ms. Smith gave the vacuum cleaner the **ultimate** test. She put it in the kids' messy playroom and turned it on.

Describe the <u>ultimate</u> model of a toy or tool you'd like to have.

_____

_____

_____

From Last to First

by John Berry

"That robot had an **uncanny** ability to get stuck in corners," said Jake. "Every time it turned around, it got stuck. Every time it threw a ball, it got stuck. Every time it moved forward or backward, it got stuck!"

Diego laughed. "I still love that robot. Sugar Ball 800. I know we're starting a new robotics season now, but she was a beauty. Remember how she nearly knocked down the principal? I thought we were doomed!"

"Thank goodness Mr. Stevens was there," said Tricia. She was talking about our team's mentor. "He explained everything. The rest of us were laughing too hard. We might have been expelled if not for Mr. Stevens."

"All SB–800 did was throw a couple of tennis balls," I said. I preferred to use the robot's formal name. "Still, I guess SB–800 did kind of run into the back of the principal's foot when it ran after the balls."

Stop Think Write

SEQUENCE OF EVENTS

Did the incident with SB-800 happen recently or a while ago? How can you tell?

_____

_____

_____

Our robotics team was meeting for the first time this year. We have fifteen members, plus Mr. Stevens, who works at an engineering company. His work focuses on **artificial** intelligence. He builds factory machines that see and think on their own. He's got exactly the right experience to mentor our team.

We named our team the RoboGorillas. Last year was not a good one for us. SB–800 got stuck in a corner at the regional games. Sarah was our radio operator. Usually, she could get SB–800 moving again, but this time a piece of wiring had gotten loose. SB–800 just kept bumping into the walls until time ran out. Our competitor scored about a thousand points, and we ended up with 125. Last place.

Stop Think Write

CAUSE AND EFFECT

Why did the RoboGorillas place last in the regional games last year?

_____

_____

_____

The Ball and Maze

We finally stopped talking about SB-800 so we could focus on *this* year's regional games. We logged onto one of the computers to find out the theme. I clicked onto the site, and there it was: "The Ball and Maze." According to the information on the site, each robot would have to move through a maze and collect balls of different sizes.

I kept reading. The maze would have hills, valleys, bridges, underpasses, and blind alleys. Two robots would compete by racing through the course, picking up balls, and putting them in a basket. The robots had just three minutes to complete the course. The more balls a robot retrieved, the more points the team would score.

"This will be tough on the robot's **sensors**," I said. I knew our robot would need to use motion and light sensors to tell different-size balls apart and to adjust movements in order to pick up the balls. I shook my head, trying to imagine all the corners where a robot could get stuck.

Stop | Think | Write

VOCABULARY

What will a robot's <u>sensors</u> need to detect in this competition?

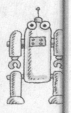

_____

_____

_____

The RoboGorillas went over all the parts we could use to build our robot. Each team gets the same parts. This year there were about 400 parts.

"Listen up," said Mr. Stevens." There have been some advances in parts since last year, which means we can build a better robot. However, we're going to have to work fast. There are just six weeks until the competition."

We spent a lot of time talking about the new central controller. The controller is like the robot's nervous system. It receives **data** from the sensors and the radio operator. For example, if a sensor shows that a corner is two feet away, the controller processes that information. If everything works right, the controller tells the robot's other parts what to do. Maybe the robot stops. Maybe it turns left. Maybe it turns around.

Stop | Think | Write

VOCABULARY

Explain what the central controller does with <u>data</u> it receives from a robot's sensors.

_____

_____

_____

247

Five weeks later...

Diego has been working hard on our new robot's tracks. SB-900 has two tracks, like a tractor. That's how the robot moves. The tracks roll. To turn, SB-900 has to tell one track to move slower or faster than the other one. Getting the tracks to move at just the right speed has been a challenge.

I've been helping with the programming. The central controller has to be told what to do. Programming requires speaking the controller's language. We've all been learning C++, the computer language that the controller understands.

The **ultimate** test is going to be the game's autonomous period. That's when each robot has to operate by itself for fifteen seconds. It can't receive any radio contact or help from its human owners, so everything needs to work perfectly.

SB–900 had a trial run today. Most parts worked well, but we still have some bugs to fix.

Stop | Think | Write

SEQUENCE OF EVENTS

What is the next thing the RoboGorillas need to do with their robot after the trial run?

_____

_____

_____

"I'm worried," Joe confided a few days later as we were walking to class.

"What are you worried about?" I asked

"I think Sugar Ball 900 is our best robot yet. I can't believe how well it picks up those balls. Diego has it turning on a dime."

"So what's the problem?" I asked.

"I'm worried about Sarah. She seems nervous because of what happened last year. We need a cool, confident radio operator. The game is too intense for an operator with a case of nerves," said Joe.

"She'll be fine," I assured him. "Sarah understands the radio better than anyone. She works with it every day." However, I was a little nervous, too. A couple of days ago, SB-900 had gotten stuck in a corner. Sarah had gotten it moving again in just six seconds, but she had looked flustered.

Stop | Think | Write

INFER AND PREDICT

Does the narrator feel absolutely confident that Sarah will be fine in the competition? How can you tell?

_____

_____

_____

The day of the competition...

"RoboGorillas," said Mr. Stevens, "I'm proud of you. Whatever happens today, you've done some fine engineering work. SB-900 is an impressive robot."

I remembered the disappointment we had felt last year. This time, I wanted us to win. We needed to advance to the national games. Our pride was at stake.

"Team RoboGorillas, are you ready?" asked the announcer. Our handlers nodded. The other team was ready, too, so the announcer said, "Let the games begin!"

The next three minutes are still a haze. Everybody was screaming. SB-900 immediately got stuck in a corner. It felt like fate. Sarah was intense, ignoring the crowd and working the radio controls. Suddenly, SB-900 turned around and picked up two balls. Before I could blink, our robot had stuffed both balls in a basket and had picked up another, a big one.

SB-900 and the RoboGorillas kept up the good work for the rest of the competition. Believe it or not, we won! Next stop: the national games.

Stop **Think** **Write**

SEQUENCE OF EVENTS

What is the first thing that happens to SB-900 at the competition?

_____

_____

_____

Look Back and Respond

1 At the first meeting of the year, what do the RoboGorillas do after they finish talking about SB-800?

_____

_____

_____

Hint

For a clue,
see page 246.

2 Why is Joe worried?

_____

_____

_____

Hint

For a clue,
see page 249.

3 How does SB-900's performance in this year's games compare to SB-800's performance in last year's games?

_____

_____

_____

Hint

For clues, see pages
245 and 250.

4 What comes next for Team RoboGorillas now that they have won "The Ball and Maze" contest?

_____

_____

_____

Hint

For a clue, see
page 250.

✓ **TARGET VOCABULARY**

innovation
menace
miraculous
tension
void

Working in Space

People have described space as an endless **1** _____. Of course, space is not empty at all. It just seems that way because of the great distances between the planets and stars. Despite the dangers, people will always want to travel into space. One way that people get there is the space shuttle.

In 1977, the space shuttle *Enterprise* was a new **2** _____ in space travel. That year, the *Enterprise* made many flights, but not into space. Instead, it stayed in Earth's atmosphere, for the purposes of tests and crew training.

The space shuttle *Columbia* was the first shuttle to fly in space. Imagine the excitement and **3** _____ that the crew must have felt just before the *Columbia* made its first trip, in 1981. The pilot on that first flight had never even been in space before. It must have seemed **4** _____ to pilot the shuttle into space and then return successfully to Earth.

Takeoff can sometimes cause damage to a space shuttle. That damage can be a **5** _____ to the flight. When the *Columbia* took off on another trip, in February of 2003, a piece of metal tore a hole in one of its wings. Despite the hole, *Columbia* made it into space. During landing, though, the craft burst into flames and broke apart. All of the crew members were killed.

An Unearthly Job

by Richard Stull

The National Aeronautics and Space Administration (NASA) is an agency of the United States government. Astronauts train for their jobs at NASA.

Today, most astronauts do their work aboard a space shuttle. They may also work at the International Space Station (ISS), a huge satellite that astronauts built in space. The astronauts flew pieces of the space station into space on the shuttle. Once in space, the astronauts put the pieces together.

Astronauts now travel back and forth between Earth and the ISS on the space shuttle. It takes two days to reach the space station from Earth.

Stop Think Write

INFER AND PREDICT

What do you think this article will mostly be about?

_____

_____

_____

An Astronaut's Work Never Ends

At the ISS, there is a lot of work to do. Astronauts unload and check supplies brought from Earth. This requires great care. A small mistake could result in a valuable piece of equipment floating off into the **void**.

Sometimes astronauts have to repair the space shuttle or the ISS. For example, they might have to repair a damaged piece of the shuttle's wing.

Working in space can be dangerous. Tiny pieces of rock called meteoroids zoom through space. These rocks can hit the astronauts as they work. Temperatures range from very hot to very cold, making space uncomfortable. There is also the possibility of exposure to harmful radiation from the sun.

Stop | Think | Write

MAIN IDEAS AND DETAILS

What is the main idea of the third paragraph? Give one detail that supports the main idea.

_____

_____

_____

Suiting Up for Safety

Astronauts wear space suits to protect their bodies. The suits are made of strong materials that are able to withstand the harsh conditions of space. The suits protect astronauts from extreme temperatures and from meteoroids.

The space suit has other uses, too. It has a helmet with a clear front that allows astronauts to see as they work. The suit is sealed, so astronauts can get oxygen. Each suit has a built-in radio that astronauts use to communicate with each other.

When astronauts need to move a short distance through space, they use a backpack with small rockets inside. Once their work outside is done, the astronauts return to the space station. They take off their space suits in a special chamber and put on regular clothes.

Stop | Think | Write

CAUSE AND EFFECT

Why must astronauts wear space suits?

_____

_____

_____

Living Without Gravity

Inside the ISS, astronauts don't walk—they float! That's because there is no gravity in space to hold things down. In space, people are weightless.

Astronauts have to be careful with water. A drop of water could become a **menace** if it floats away and jams up an expensive computer. Water, crumbs, and even lint must be carefully contained at all times.

Sleeping in space is one of the easiest things to do. Astronauts can sleep anywhere because they are weightless. They can sleep upside down or float around the cabin. Some astronauts strap themselves into a sleeping bag attached to a wall. Others just fasten a pillow around their heads. Most astronauts sleep for eight hours a night.

Stop | Think | Write

VOCABULARY

Why does the author describe a floating drop of water as a <u>menace</u>?

_____

_____

_____

Daily Life on the ISS

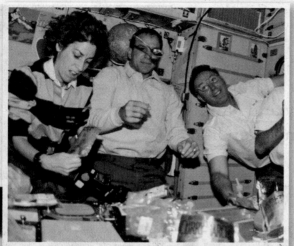

Astronauts bring food and water with them when they go into space. They store food in a kitchen on the ISS. Like most kitchens, it has a stove and a refrigerator.

Astronauts eat what most people eat, but they prepare their meals differently. Most of their food has had all water removed from it. The dried food comes sealed in packets that weigh very little and don't take up much space. To make a meal, the astronauts add water to the contents of a packet. Then they heat it up and eat the food directly from the packet.

Astronauts must dine carefully in space. That's because their food can easily float away. Just as astronauts can float across the room, so too can food and utensils!

Stop Think Write

MAIN IDEAS AND DETAILS

Which details support the main idea that astronauts prepare food differently from most people?

_____

_____

_____

Free Time in Space

Astronauts do not have much free time in space, but they do relax sometimes. They might read a book or send e-mail to a family member. They might also play an instrument or take photographs of things outside the windows. There are lots of **miraculous** sights in space!

Astronauts must exercise every day to keep their muscles strong and their bones healthy. Keeping fit and having fun help crew members avoid **tension** during space shuttle flights.

Stop | Think | Write

VOCABULARY

What kinds of <u>miraculous</u> sights do you think astronauts see from the space station?

_____

_____

_____

How Work in Space Helps Life on Earth

Astronauts spend most of their time in space working. Some study the effects of weightlessness or test a new computer **innovation**. Others conduct experiments, such as testing the growth of seeds in space, or the human body's reaction to being in space. Still others study what Earth looks like from space.

The work astronauts do is important to our understanding of life on Earth. For example, astronauts can measure changes in polar caps, and this helps us to understand the effects of global warming. Astronauts' work also provides information about other planets and stars that are our neighbors in space.

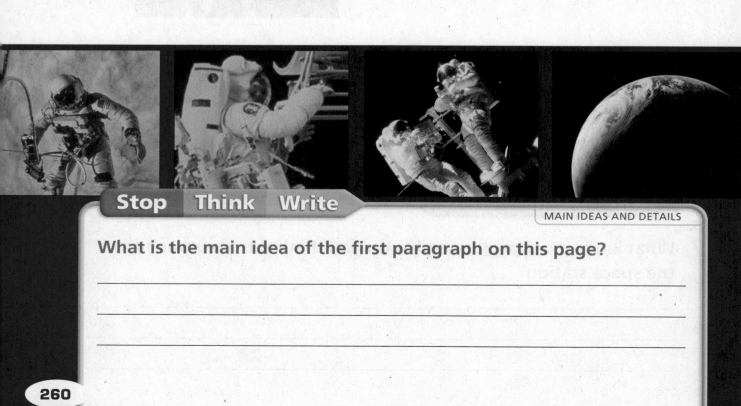

Stop **Think** **Write**

MAIN IDEAS AND DETAILS

What is the main idea of the first paragraph on this page?

_____

_____

_____

Look Back and Respond

1 **What is this article mainly about?**

_____

_____

_____

Hint

You can find clues on almost every page.

2 **How does weightlessness affect the lives of the astronauts in space?**

_____

_____

_____

Hint

For clues, see pages 257, 258, and 259.

3 **What details support the main idea that astronauts work hard?**

_____

_____

_____

Hint

For clues, see pages 254, 255, and 260.

4 **Why is the work astronauts do in space important to life on Earth?**

_____

_____

_____

Hint

For clues, see page 260.

Lesson 27

✓ TARGET VOCABULARY

consequences
frigid
intense
retains
venture

Mountaintops

1 The air is **frigid** on high mountaintops during much of the year. The cold can be as extreme as that in the Arctic.

Describe the most <u>frigid</u> place you have visited.

_____

_____

_____

2 Winds can be very **intense** on mountaintops. In a 1934 storm, wind gusted over New Hampshire's Mt. Washington at 231 miles per hour!

What is the most <u>intense</u> weather you have experienced?

_____

_____

_____

3 A high mountain peak **retains** its original wildlife. Few people visit, so plants and animals aren't disturbed.

Describe something that <u>retains</u> its shape after you use it.

_____

_____

_____

4 Many mountains have glaciers, which are giant rivers of ice. One of the **consequences** of global warming is the melting of glaciers.

What are the <u>consequences</u> of a big storm?

_____

_____

_____

5 Few people will **venture** to the peaks of the world's tallest mountains. The dangers at such heights are too great for most of us.

What is something that you would <u>venture</u> to do?

_____

_____

_____

The Arctic: A Melting Ocean

by John Berry

Imagine walking on top of an ocean. Believe it or not, there is an ocean you can walk on! It is the Arctic Ocean. Sadly, we may not be able to walk on it in the future.

The Arctic Ocean surrounds the North Pole. It is the world's smallest ocean. Thick ice covers most of the Arctic Ocean. In some places, the ice is twenty feet thick or more.

Scientists who study this unusual ocean observe animals that live on top of and below the ice. They also study the ice itself. They measure and drill, taking samples from deep within.

Scientists have discovered that the ice cover is changing. There is less of it than there used to be. Scientists believe this may be one of the **consequences** of global warming.

Stop Think Write

CONCLUSIONS AND GENERALIZATIONS

What conclusion have scientists drawn about why ice in the Arctic Ocean is thinning?

_____

_____

_____

The Ice Zone

The Arctic Ocean has two parts: the ice zone and the water zone. The ice zone consists of frozen seawater, snowdrifts, and ridges and walls of ice. There are even mountains of ice.

Despite the **intense** cold, many animals live in the ice zone, including hares, polar bears, birds, and seals. These animals have learned how to live on the ice.

There is life within the ice, too. Tiny one-cell plants live deep in the ice. They are so small that you can only see them with a microscope.

The ice zone isn't always the same size. It changes during the year. In the summer, when the air heats up, the water below the ice becomes warmer. As a result, pools of water form on the surface of the ice, cracks appear, and some of the ice splits apart.

Stop | Think | Write

CAUSE AND EFFECT

What causes pools of water to form on the surface of the ice?

_____

_____

_____

A Freezing Cold Sea

The Arctic Ocean goes down 4,000 feet in some places. That may sound deep, but the Arctic is actually the shallowest ocean on Earth.

The Arctic's **frigid** water stays within a few degrees of freezing. Divers say that the water feels thicker than normal seawater. That's because it's almost frozen. If you were to stick just one finger in the Arctic, you'd jump back from the cold.

Surprisingly, many creatures live in the Arctic Ocean. Some fish thrive here, such as the Arctic cod. You can also find crabs, starfish, and sea cucumbers crawling along the ocean floor.

Some whales live in the Arctic Ocean, too, including the narwhal. Nicknamed the "unicorn of the sea," the male narwhal has a single tusk on the front of its head that can grow to more than nine feet long!

Stop **Think** **Write**

CONCLUSIONS AND GENERALIZATIONS

Why is it surprising that many creatures live in the Arctic Ocean?

_____

_____

_____

A Changing Sea

Canadian scientist Roy Koerner has spent time studying the Arctic Ocean and walking on its ice. In 1969, he made the ultimate trip. He and three others were brave enough to **venture** all the way across the Arctic Ocean on dogsleds.

Koerner's trip would not be possible today. That's because the ocean has changed. The water zone is growing, while the ice zone is shrinking. There is less ice now than at any time since people began keeping records. In some places, the ice is half as thick as it used to be.

Some say the changes are due to global warming. Global warming affects many places. However, scientists claim it's happening as much as seven times faster in the Arctic than in other areas. Much has changed since Koerner began his study of the Arctic. He describes today's Arctic Ocean as "a different world."

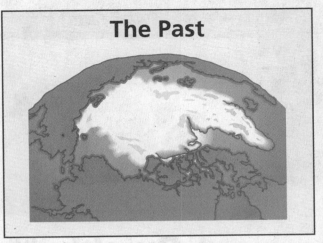

The Past

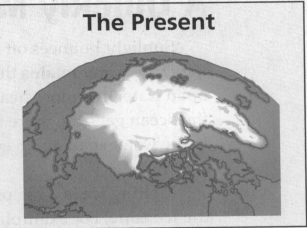

The Present

The Future

Stop · Think · Write

VOCABULARY

Why did it take bravery to <u>venture</u> across the Arctic Ocean?

_____

_____

_____

A Quickly Melting Ocean

Sunlight bounces off ice, but ocean water absorbs light. The water **retains** the heat from sunlight. The more open water, the more heat the ocean captures. The warmer the ocean gets, the more the ice melts, which results in the water soaking up even more sunlight. The cycle continues.

Melting ice is a big problem for animals living in the ice zone. For example, polar bears have adapted to life on the ice. Layers of blubber keep them warm, pads on their feet keep them from slipping on ice, and their white color helps them blend in. Polar bears aren't just suited for the ice—they need it. They use ice for hunting. They wait next to holes in the ice for seals to come up for air. When a seal comes up, a polar bear catches its meal. Without the ice, hunting is almost impossible. According to scientists, polar bears may be extinct within a hundred years.

Stop | Think | Write

VOCABULARY

What happens when open water in the Arctic <u>retains</u> the sun's heat?

_____

_____

_____

Effects on People

Melting ice affects more than just animals in the Arctic. It affects people, too. Many people live near the ocean's edge. Ice near the shore protects their villages by stopping the waves from coming ashore during storms.

The shrinking ice is a threat to villages. Waves wear down the shorelines and cause the ground to fall into the sea. Over time, the ocean moves inland. In some villages, the sea is turning homes into debris. When the shoreline crumbles, homes along its edge crash into the water.

For people living in the Arctic, the melting ocean is a terrible problem. Many have to leave the villages that their ancestors built and start over somewhere else.

Stop | **Think** | **Write**

CAUSE AND EFFECT

How does the loss of ice affect Arctic villages?

_____

_____

_____

Adapting to Change

Despite the damage caused by melting ice, the people of the Arctic are making the best of climate change. For example, more areas of open water make it easier to fish. Open water also makes travel and shipping easier and quicker.

Long ago, explorers and merchants dreamed of a Northwest Passage through the Arctic Ocean. They thought the passage would begin in the Atlantic Ocean, go through the Arctic, and end at the Pacific Ocean. The dream has never come true because ice has always blocked the way. Soon, however, this may change.

Scientists do not know exactly what will happen to the Arctic Ocean. One thing is certain, though. Scientists such as Roy Koerner will be keeping a close watch on this changing sea.

Stop | Think | Write

CONCLUSIONS AND GENERALIZATIONS

How could the dream of a Northwest Passage finally become a reality?

_____

_____

_____

Look Back and Respond

1 Scientist Roy Koerner concluded that the Arctic Ocean is "a different world" today. What evidence supports his conclusion?

_____

_____

_____

Hint

For a clue, see page 267.

2 Overall, would an ice-free Arctic Ocean be good for animals that live in the ice zone? Explain.

_____

_____

_____

Hint

For a clue, see page 268.

3 What general statement can you make about the effects of the melting ocean on the people who live in the Arctic?

_____

_____

_____

Hint

For a clue, see page 269

4 How could global warming help fishermen?

_____

_____

_____

Hint

For a clue, see page 270.

affirmed
deduced
motive
mounting
perilous

Butterfly Watching

1 Observing some animals in nature can be **perilous**. Luckily, butterfly watching is not. It is both fun and safe to observe butterflies in their natural habitat.

Describe a <u>perilous</u> animal-watching situation.

_____

_____

_____

2 There are more butterflies in Texas than anywhere else in the United States. You can see many different types at the International Butterfly Park, in the Rio Grande Valley. One **motive** for creating the park was to teach people about butterflies.

What <u>motive</u> could a visitor have to visit the **International Butterfly Park?**

_____

_____

3 One butterfly watcher was keeping a checklist of butterflies that she observed. She felt her excitement **mounting** every time she saw a new kind of butterfly.

Think about bird watching, another popular hobby. What might cause a bird watcher to feel <u>mounting</u> excitement?

_____

_____

_____

4 The butterfly watcher came upon a large orange butterfly with black markings. Based on what she remembered about butterflies, she **deduced** that it was a Monarch butterfly.

Write a synonym for <u>deduced</u>.

_____

5 The butterfly watcher looked at her guidebook and found a picture of the butterfly she was observing. She **affirmed** that it was indeed a Monarch butterfly.

What did the butterfly watcher see that <u>affirmed</u> her prediction that the butterfly was a Monarch?

_____

_____

_____

Jay's Butterflies

by Margaret Maugenest

Jay Jackson and Mattie Helm sit next to each other in class. Jay is enthusiastic about butterflies. He takes his butterfly field guide with him everywhere he goes.

"Why are you always lugging that book around?" asked Mattie one day.

"I like to study the pictures," he answered. "That way, when I see a butterfly, I know what kind it is."

Mattie rolled her eyes and made a yawning motion with her hand over her mouth. "I can't think of anything more BO-RING!"

Jay shrugged his shoulders. "Well, you'd be surprised by how many different butterflies there are around here," he told her. He would have told her more, but Mattie wasn't really listening. She was busy sending a text message to her friend Sally about where to meet after school.

Stop | **Think** | **Write**

How does Mattie feel about Jay's hobby? How can you tell?

_____

_____

_____

The following day was Saturday, and Jay did what he always did on the weekend. He packed up his field guide, binoculars, notepad, camera, water, protein bar, and apple. The digital camera was a birthday gift from his Aunt Lucy. The zoom lens was great for taking close-up photos of butterflies and other creatures.

"What are you hoping to find today?" his mom asked. She knew where he was going.

"I really hope I see a Swallowtail," said Jay on his way out the door.

"Good luck!" she called after him. She was happy to know that her son was spending time outdoors in the fresh air.

Stop | Think | Write

UNDERSTANDING CHARACTERS

What is Jay like? How can you tell?

_____

_____

_____

275

Jay strapped on his bike helmet and headed to the nature preserve. Rather than take a **perilous** ride through busy streets, Jay took the safer back roads. When he got to the preserve, he parked his bike by the entrance.

Ranger Rogers was sitting in his booth. "Back again for the butterflies?" he asked Jay knowingly.

Jay nodded and smiled. He started up the hiking trail that wound through the woods of cypress and oak trees. The trail opened into a huge, colorful field filled with wildflowers and milkweed plants—a perfect spot for butterfly watching. Jay had always been lucky here. He thought about the Dusky Wing butterflies that he had seen just last week.

Stop   Think   Write

What could make streets **perilous** for bike riders?

_____

_____

_____

Jay breathed in the fresh air. He looked up at the clear blue sky, and felt the warm sun shining down. A gentle breeze rustled through the grasses and plants.

Watching butterflies took time and patience, but Jay liked that about his hobby. Spending time in nature was one **motive** Jay had for watching butterflies. Looking for interesting butterflies was also like a treasure hunt. His treasure was seeing a butterfly, looking at it closely for its shape, color, and markings, and finally identifying it. He usually tried to take some pictures. Jay was proud of his collection of butterfly photographs.

He took out his binoculars and camera and put them around his neck for quick and easy access. He listened to two songbirds twittering and watched them flit from tree to tree. Jay observed the birds through his binoculars and then scanned the field to see what insects were hovering nearby.

Stop | Think | Write

VOCABULARY

What is Jay's <u>motive</u> for pulling out his binoculars?

_____

_____

_____

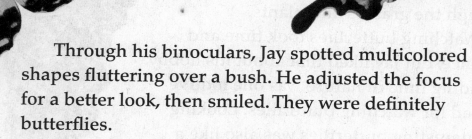

Through his binoculars, Jay spotted multicolored shapes fluttering over a bush. He adjusted the focus for a better look, then smiled. They were definitely butterflies.

As Jay walked in their direction, he came upon two black and yellow butterflies dancing in the breeze. Jay kept his eyes on them while pulling out his camera. When one butterfly landed on a flower, Jay snuck up to it. He moved as quietly as possible, and snapped a picture. Jay zoomed in on the butterfly to get a shot of it sucking up the sweet nectar inside the flower. Its striped wings were folded.

Jay felt his excitement **mounting** when he noticed the tail shape at the end of the butterfly's wings. From the markings, and the tail, he **deduced** that this was a Tiger Swallowtail. Jay held his breath. He hoped that he could get a clear photograph. He waited for the exact moment. Just as the butterfly opened its wings, Jay clicked the camera. He got the shot he wanted!

Stop Think Write

UNDERSTANDING CHARACTERS

How can you tell that Jay is a good photographer?

_____

_____

_____

Back at home, Jay downloaded the pictures from his camera to his laptop. He didn't like to capture butterflies and mount them, because that meant the butterflies would die. Taking photos caused no harm to the butterflies.

Comparing his photographs of the Tiger Swallowtail with the pictures in the field guide, Jay **affirmed** that his find was indeed a Swallowtail. He was so excited. It was exactly the butterfly he'd been hoping to see! He showed his parents the photo.

"You said you hoped you would see a Swallowtail, and you did!" said his mom. "I'm happy for you."

"Yep, me too," said his dad. "Life's like that, Jay. Sometimes you get lucky!"

Stop Think Write

CONCLUSIONS AND GENERALIZATIONS

How is Jay's way of butterfly collecting better than capturing real butterflies?

_____

_____

_____

Jay thought about Mattie, specifically about how she had told him that butterfly watching was boring. "I'll show her," he thought. He printed out a photograph just for her, and he put it in an envelope.

On Monday, Jay handed the envelope to Mattie just as she got to her desk. "See what I found over the weekend," he said proudly.

Mattie took the envelope. "For me?" she asked, opening it. Jay watched her. He couldn't help but notice her eyes light up and a little smile come over her face.

"You took this picture?" she asked.

"Who else?" he answered.

"Not bad. Thanks," she said. Then she carefully put the picture back in the envelope and placed it in her desk.

Stop **Think** **Write**

UNDERSTANDING CHARACTERS

Why do you think Jay gives Mattie the picture?

_____

_____

_____

Look Back and Respond

1 How can you tell that Jay doesn't mind doing things by himself?

_____

_____

_____

Hint

Clues you can use are on almost every page!

2 Give three examples in the story that show how Jay is observant, that he looks at things carefully.

_____

_____

_____

Hint

For clues, see pages 277, 278, and 279.

3 How do Jay's parents feel about his butterfly watching?

_____

_____

_____

Hint

For clues, see pages 275 and 279.

4 Do you think Mattie changes her mind about butterflies? Explain.

_____

_____

_____

Hint

For clues, see pages 274 and 280.

destiny
embrace
majestic
massive
temperaments

About Whales

Whales are beautiful, **majestic** mammals that live in the sea. Some are **massive**. For example, the blue whale can grow to be over 90 feet long and over 150 tons. That's as big as a nine-story building. In fact, the blue whale is the largest animal on Earth.

Despite their huge size, whales are difficult to spot. If you should see one, **embrace** the moment. Sadly, the **destiny** of these amazing creatures does not look good. The humpback whale is just one of several species in danger of becoming extinct.

Legends describe whales as gentle giants. For example, even though orcas are called "killer whales," their **temperaments** are not very aggressive.

1 Some whales are small, but most are

_____.

2 If you see a humpback whale,

_____ the moment, as these are

endangered animals.

3 Surprisingly, killer whales do not have very

aggressive _____.

4 What is the most majestic sight you have ever

seen? What made it so special?

_____

_____

_____

5 Why might endangered animals have a sad

destiny?

_____

_____

_____

283

Giants of the Sea

by Mia Lewis

Whales are among the most fascinating and amazing creatures on the planet. Their **majestic** size, grace, and intelligence set them apart from other animals. Don't pass up a chance to see whales for yourself.

Whale watching requires great patience. You will see more waves than whales, and you may spend most of the time scanning the horizon. However, the moment you spot your first whale, you'll feel that all the hours of searching were worth it.

Whales do the most amazing things. They "spy-hop," resting vertically while popping their heads up above the water to look around. They "lob-tail," lifting their enormous tails into the air and bringing them down with a loud splat. They "breach," jumping right out of the water. Watching whales perform is a show you do not want to miss.

Stop Think Write

PERSUASION

How does the author try to persuade readers to see whales for themselves?

_____

_____

_____

Whales Breathe and Birth Like Humans

Whales may live in the sea, but they are mammals, like humans. Whales breathe into their lungs, just as we do, coming to the surface from time to time to get air. Not many mammals live in the sea. Whales are unusual in this way.

Instead of having a nose with nostrils, a whale has a blowhole at the top of its head. When the blowhole appears above the surface of the water, a fountain of water may shoot high into the sky.

Whales give birth to live young, like other mammals. They have just one baby, or calf, at a time. The calf can swim as soon as it is born in order to keep up with its mother. The mother nurses the calf with rich milk, which is high in fat content, to keep her baby warm in the cold waters.

Like other mammals, whales are warm-blooded. Even without hair or fur, they maintain a steady body temperature. A thick layer of fat right under the skin, called blubber, helps whales maintain their body heat.

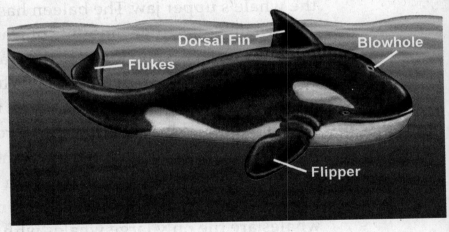

Dorsal Fin

Flukes

Blowhole

Flipper

Stop | Think | Write

COMPARE AND CONTRAST

How are whales like humans? How are they different?

_____

_____

_____

A baleen whale

A toothed whale

Not All Whales Are the Same

There are seventy-six species of whales, and they can be divided into two main groups: *baleen* (no teeth) and *toothed*. The biggest whales are baleen. Surprisingly, these massive creatures have no teeth!

Instead of teeth, baleen whales have "baleen plates," that work like strainers. Baleen is a hard but elastic substance that looks like a comb hanging from the whale's upper jaw. The baleen has hairy bristles. The whale gulps huge amounts of water as it swims near the surface. Then it forces the water out of its mouth, through the baleen plates. When small food organisms are caught on the bristles, the whale uses its tongue to guide them down its throat. It takes a lot of straining and slurping to make a meal!

Most whales, however, have teeth and are smaller. Killer whales (which are also called orcas) and sperm whales are the only large whales with teeth.

Stop **Think** **Write**

INFER AND PREDICT

Why does the author find it surprising that baleen whales have no teeth?

_____

_____

_____

Whales on Show

Some whales live in captivity in marine parks, where they perform in shows. Killer whales are among the most popular attractions.

Skilled trainers work with the mammals to teach them "tricks." Killer whales' even and acrobatic **temperaments** make them well suited to participate in marine park shows. However, a whale is still an animal and therefore unpredictable. As much as you may want to **embrace** a whale, it is dangerous for anyone but a trainer to make contact.

The shows are fun, but some people disapprove of them because the whales in shows are captive. They feel that no matter how good the conditions are, it is not fair to keep a whale out of its natural habitat. Whales were born to be free.

Stop Think Write

VOCABULARY

Why could it be dangerous to <u>embrace</u> a whale?

_____

_____

_____

Whale
hunters at work

Whale Hunting

For thousands of years, people have hunted whales
for everything from meat for food to oil for lamps.
Whale hunting, or whaling, has been a terrible threat
to the world's whales. Hunters killed so many whales
during the first half of the 20th century that today many
species are close to extinct.

The International Whaling Commission (IWC)
banned most commercial whaling in 1986. However,
some native peoples have permission to kill a specific
number of whales each year to help preserve their
traditional cultures.

Not all countries are members of the IWC. Some
non-member countries continue to hunt whales.
They say that a controlled amount of whaling is safe.
However, only a complete ban will stop the cruelty to
these magnificent creatures.

Stop Think Write

PERSUASION

How do you think the author wants the reader to feel about
whaling? How can you tell?

_____

_____

_____

Helping Whales

Despite the general ban on whaling, whales are still in danger. Accidents cause more whale deaths than hunting. Ships, for example, accidentally kill many whales each year. There should be laws to make ships slow down in areas where whales live and travel.

Hitting whales with ships is just one way that humans harm these wonderful creatures. Many whales also die getting tangled in nets set out by fishermen. Pollution, climate change, and too much noise are bad for whales, too.

The **destiny** of whales is in our hands. We must work to find solutions to the problems that threaten this amazing animal. If we don't, many species of whales may become extinct. Once a species of whale is extinct, it is gone forever. It would be sad to think of a world without whales.

Stop | Think | Write

PERSUASION

How does the author try to persuade the reader that it is important to protect whales?

_____

_____

_____

Whale

Q&A

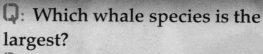

Q: Which whale species is the largest?

A: The largest whale is the blue whale. It can grow to over 90 feet long, and weigh over 150 tons! Blue whales are an endangered species.

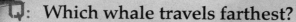

Q: Which whale travels farthest?

A: Gray whales migrate as far as 12,500 miles each year. In the summer, they feed in the cold Arctic waters. They give birth to their young in the warm waters off Baja California. They often travel close to the coast. Thousands of people go to see them pass by in the spring and fall.

Q: Which whale is most at risk of becoming extinct?

A: The northern right whale is the most endangered of all whales. It lives along the Atlantic coast of North America. Only about 350 of these whales remain.

Stop | Think | Write

AUTHOR'S PURPOSE

Why do you think the author gives information about blue whales and northern right whales being endangered?

_____

_____

_____

Look Back and Respond

1 What are the two main groups of whales? Which group do most whales belong to?

_____

_____

_____

Hint

Look for clues on page 286.

2 What argument does the author use to persuade the reader that it is cruel to keep whales in marine parks?

_____

_____

Hint

For a clue, see page 287.

3 Why does the IWC allow some native groups to hunt some whales each year?

_____

_____

_____

Hint

For a clue, see page 288.

4 Write two details about gray whales that you can find in this article.

_____

_____

_____

Hint

For clues, see page 290.

✓ **TARGET VOCABULARY**

conditions
data
intently
jeopardy
subsided

Hurricane Danger

1 During a hurricane, weather **conditions** become very dangerous. High winds and floods damage property and threaten human life.

How might hurricane <u>conditions</u> be dangerous to a person?

_____

_____

_____

2 Weather forecasters track hurricanes. They collect **data** about a storm's speed and location. These facts help forcasters decide if a hurricane is dangerous.

What tools might scientists use to collect <u>data</u> about a hurricane?

_____

_____

_____

3 When a hurricane approaches, forecasters follow it **intently**. They watch closely to learn its path and predict where it will land.

When might you need to follow events intently?

_____

_____

_____

4 A hurricane can place an entire city in **jeopardy**. Forecasters must warn people about approaching storms so they can get out of harm's way.

Tell about a time when you felt that you were in jeopardy.

_____

_____

_____

5 After a bad hurricane, when the winds and high water have **subsided**, the cleanup begins. People work hard to get their homes, and their lives, back in order again.

Why must people wait until winds have subsided before they can clean up?

_____

_____

_____

The Worst Hurricane Ever

by Duncan Searl

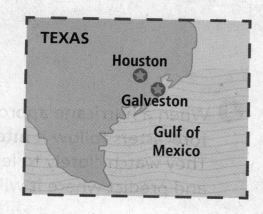

TEXAS
Houston
Galveston
Gulf of Mexico

In 1900, the city of Galveston was booming. With a population of 42,000, it was the largest city in Texas. Galveston boasted electric lights, streetcars, concert halls, luxury hotels, and long-distance telephones.

Trade made the city rich. Ships from around the world docked at Galveston Bay, a natural harbor. The location, however, made some people nervous. Built on a low island in the bay, some citizens wanted to build a seawall around Galveston to protect it from hurricanes.

The United States Weather Bureau thought that a seawall was not necessary. They assured the people of Galveston that there was nothing to worry about.

Scientists believed that the floor of the Gulf of Mexico, which slopes gradually away from Galveston, would stop hurricanes from forming there. Today we know this is not true.

Stop | Think | Write

TEXT AND GRAPHIC FEATURES

Look at the map. How does Galveston's location make the city vulnerable to hurricanes?

_____

_____

_____

A Reason to Worry

On September 8, 1900, the people of Galveston awoke to a surprising sight: several inches of water running down their streets. What they saw wasn't rain—it was seawater!

Children splashed in the water and sailed toy boats. Crowds walked down to the beach. High waves crashed against the seafront shops.

Everyone knew a storm was coming, but people were not worried. Storms were fairly common, and most did not cause much damage.

However, on the Gulf of Mexico, the captain of the *Pensacola* was worried. He had just sailed out of Galveston into a terrible hurricane. High waves crashed over his steamship, and 120-mile-per-hour winds tore away the anchor.

The hurricane was heading straight for Galveston, but the captain had no way of warning the city. Ship radios were a new invention, and the *Pensacola* didn't have one.

Stop Think Write

TEXT AND GRAPHIC FEATURES

Look at the head *A Reason to Worry*. How does it hint at the effect the hurricane will have on Galveston?

_____

_____

_____

Conditions Worsen

Weather forecasters in Cuba were worried, too. A storm passed over that island on September 4. The forecasters watched it **intently** and reported that the storm was curving into the Gulf of Mexico.

Weather officials in Washington, D.C., got the report from Cuba, but they didn't believe it. They thought the storm was moving up the Atlantic coast. Remember, storm forecasting was a new science in 1900. With no satellites or airplanes, collecting **data** on hurricanes was difficult. There was no radar, either, making it impossible to track storms closely.

The officials didn't want to make a mistake. A false hurricane warning was costly and embarrassing, so officials posted no warnings for the Gulf of Mexico.

Meanwhile, people in Galveston watched nervously as water continued to rise.

Stop Think Write

CAUSE AND EFFECT

Why didn't weather officials give warnings for the Gulf of Mexico about the hurricane?

_____

_____

_____

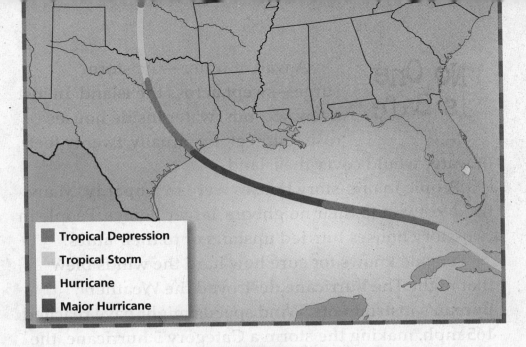

Tropical Depression
Tropical Storm
Hurricane
Major Hurricane

Disaster Strikes!

Conditions on the island worsened. The water rose steadily, the winds picked up, and a heavy rain began.

Wind tore down the telegraph and telephone lines, cutting off communication with the mainland. No one outside Galveston knew what was happening. Railroad lines from the city were soon underwater, making it impossible to leave. There was no escape.

The Weather Service used special flags for hurricane warnings. Officials never raised those flags in Galveston, though. Most people still thought they would be safe at home. Only a few went to schools and churches for safety.

At 7:30 P.M., the hurricane made landfall. It was a direct hit on Galveston.

Stop | Think | Write

TEXT AND GRAPHIC FEATURES

How does the map on this page help you understand the power of the hurricane that hit Galveston?

_____

_____

_____

No One Is Safe

A wall of water—the storm surge—swept across the island. In just a few seconds, water inside houses rose four feet. Eventually, twenty feet of water would cover the island.

People in one-story houses were in **jeopardy**. Many tried to swim to their neighbors' larger homes. People in two-story houses hurried upstairs or to their attics.

No one knows for sure how hard the winds blew that night. The hurricane destroyed the Weather Bureau's instruments. Wind speeds might have reached 165 mph, making the storm a Category 5 hurricane, the most dangerous and destructive kind.

The buildings along the Gulf Coast fell first. In the high winds, shingles and boards became missiles. Even telephone poles flew through the air. No one was safe from the flying objects.

Stop | Think | Write

VOCABULARY

Describe two ways that the people of Galveston were in jeopardy.

_____

_____

_____

The Damage

A mountain of wreckage formed near the beach. Pushed by winds and water, debris moved across the island. As the wreckage moved, it grew. Like a giant bulldozer, it leveled much of Galveston.

The side of the island facing the Gulf of Mexico suffered most. Even the strongest houses there could not stand up to the winds and water. Eventually, the houses broke apart.

Terrified families floated off with their houses. People clung to doors, walls, and roofs. In the rain and darkness, they had no idea where they were. Their neighborhoods were gone. Galveston was now part of the Gulf of Mexico.

Finally, during the night, the winds **subsided**. The water slowly flowed back into the sea.

Damaged homes and debris after a hurricane.

Stop Think Write

VOCABULARY

How do you think the survivors felt when the winds finally <u>subsided</u>?

_____

_____

_____

The Aftermath

When the sun rose the next day, survivors couldn't believe their eyes. The hurricane had destroyed 3,600 buildings. A tangled mass of broken boards, furniture, and personal belongings covered much of the island.

The deadly hurricane killed at least 7,000 people, making it the worst natural disaster to strike the United States.

In the years that followed, the people of Galveston rebuilt their city. Soon, there were new railroads, concert halls, and luxury hotels. The pride of Galveston, however, was its new seventeen-foot seawall.

Since 1900, the seawall has protected the city from many hurricanes. In addition, modern technology now lets scientists track storms more accurately, enabling them to alert cities to hurricanes days ahead of time. Storm warnings give people time to move to safety—and make it unlikely that Galveston will ever suffer such terrible losses from a hurricane again.

Stop **Think** **Write**

MAIN IDEAS AND DETAILS

After the 1900 hurricane, what did the people of Galveston do to protect their city from future storms?

_____

_____

_____

Look Back and Respond

1 Think about the title of this article. What does it tell you about the Galveston hurricane?

Hint
Clues you can use are on pages 298, 299, and 300.

_____

_____

_____

2 How does the photograph on page 299 help you understand what hurricanes can do?

Hint
What do you see in the photograph?

_____

_____

_____

3 Do you think the job of rebuilding Galveston after the hurricane was easy, kind of difficult, or very difficult? Explain.

Hint
Clues you can use are on page 300.

_____

_____

_____

4 How are people better able to prepare for hurricanes today than they were in 1900?

Hint
Clues you can use are on pages 296 and 300.

_____

_____

_____

Summarize Strategy

When you **summarize**, briefly retell the important ideas in a text.

- Use your own words.

- Organize ideas in a way that makes sense.

- Do not change the meaning of the text.

- Make your summary short. Use only a few sentences.

When you **paraphrase**, restate the author's words in a new way. A paraphrase can be about as long as the text.

- Use synonyms.

- Change the order of words in a sentence.

- Combine sentences. Put related ideas together.

Analyze/Evaluate Strategy

You can **analyze** and **evaluate** a text. Study the text carefully. Then form an opinion about it.

1. Analyze the text. Look at the ideas. Think about what the author tells you.
   - What are the important facts and details?
   - How are the ideas organized?
   - What does the author want you to know?

2. Evaluate the text. Decide what is important. Then form an opinion.
   - How do you feel about what you read?
   - Do you agree with the author's ideas?
   - Did the author succeed in reaching his or her goals?

Infer/Predict Strategy

You can make an **inference**. Figure out what the author does not tell you.

• Think about the clues in the text.

• Think about what you already know.

You can make a **prediction**. Use text clues to figure out what will happen next.

Monitor/Clarify Strategy

You can **monitor** what you read. Pay attention to how well you understand the text.

If you read a part that doesn't make sense, find a way to **clarify** it. Clear up what you don't understand.

• Use what you already know.

• Reread or read ahead. Find clues in the text.

• Read more slowly.

• Ask questions about the text.

Question Strategy

Ask yourself **questions** before, during, and after you read. Look for answers.

Some questions to ask:
- What does the author mean here?
- Who or what is this about?
- Why did this happen?
- What is the main idea?
- How does this work?

Visualize Strategy

You can **visualize** as you read. Use text details to make pictures in your mind.
- Use the author's words and your own knowledge to help.
- Make mental pictures of people, places, things, actions, and ideas.

PHOTO CREDITS